ARCANA

ARCANA
A Stephen Jonas Reader

Edited by Garrett Caples, Derek Fenner,
David Rich, & Joseph Torra

City Lights Books | San Francisco

ISBN: 978-08-72867-91-8

Library of Congress Cataloging-in-Publication Data
Names: Jonas, Stephen, author. | Caples, Garrett T., editor. | Fenner, Derek, editor.
 | Rich, David, 1979- editor. | Torra, Joseph, 1955- editor.
Title: Arcana : a Stephen Jonas reader / edited by Garrett Caples, Derek
 Fenner, David Rich, & Joseph Torra.
Description: San Francisco : City Lights Books, 2019. | Includes previously
 uncollected and unpublished work, a section of never-before-seen
 facsimiles from notebooks, and a generous selection from his innovative
 serial poem "Exercises for Ear" (1968); with an introduction by Joseph
 Torra. | Includes bibliographical references.
Identifiers: LCCN 2018057264 | ISBN 9780872867918 (alk. paper)
Classification: LCC PS3560.O45 A6 2019 | DDC 821/.914--dc23
LC record available at https://lccn.loc.gov/2018057264

City Lights would like to thank Joel Tomfohr for production assistance.

City Lights books are published at the City Lights Bookstore
261 Columbus Avenue, San Francisco, CA 94133.
Visit our website: www.citylights.com

Contents

Editorial Note – 13

Introduction – 17

Published Poems – 29
    Invocation – 31
    . . . . . An Ear Injured by Hearing Things (after a statement
        of Jack Spicer's) – 32
    The Outraged Genius – 34
    Blackstone Park (Dans le vieux parc solitaire et glacé) – 35
    Subway Haiku – 36
    The Celibate – 40
    Brisk Walk to Pavilion of Good Crops & Peace (Three
        Versions from the Chinese) – 41
    Green – 43
    Tensone with Relent – 44
    Three Dance Moods for Ear – 45
    The Return – 47
    from Orgasms/Dominations – 48
        I – 48
        II – 51
        III – 55
        IV – 59
        V – 62
        XXXIII – 67
    Canto Jondo for Soul Brother Jack Spicer, His Beloved
        California & Andalusia of Lorca – 70
    Gloucester (Impressions for J.W., III) – 75
    Complainte de L'Oubli des Morts – 77
    The Street – 78
    Brotherhood & All That Bad Air – 79
    Morphogenesis (being a conventionalization "Morphemes"
        of Jack Spicer) – 80
    Back 'O Town Blues – 84
    Dilemma II – 85
    For John Wieners 1/6/60 – 87
    Word on Measure – 89
    The Music Master (after a Mozart divertimento) – 92
    A Theme – 94
    Fragmentum, 1957 – 95
    Following the Same Route but at a Different Pace – 96

4 Poems of Myself & Others – 97

A Revel (for John Fusco) – 100

A Widow's Lament (after the Chinese) – 103

What Made Maude Hum – 104

To a Strayed Cat – 109

Song After Waller, Herrick & Others – 110

To Strum Ole Homer's Lute – 111

Song of Myself – 112

Love, the Poem, the Sea & Other Pieces Examined
     by Me – 113

One of Three Musicians – 117

For Leroi Jones – 118

A Proposition (for Ed Marshall) – 119

An Ode for Garcia Lorca – 121

Ornithic Scene – 122

from Exercises for Ear – 123

       I, III – 125

       IV, V, IX –126

       X, XII – 127

       XIV, XVI, XVIII – 128

       XIX, XX – 129

       XXII, XXIII – 130

       XXIV, XXVI – 131

       XXVIII, XXIX, XXX – 132

       XXXIII, XXXIV – 133

       XXXV, XXXVI, XXXVII – 134

       XXXVIII, XXXIX – 135

       XLI, XLII –136

       XLIII, XLV – 137

       XLVII, XLVIII – 138

       L – 139

       LI, LV – 140

       LX, LXI – 141

       LXII, LXIII, LXIV – 142

       LXV –143

       LXVII, LXVIII, LXIX – 144

       LXXIV, LXXVII – 145

       LXXIX, LXXX – 146

       LXXXII, LXXXIV – 147

       LXXXV, LXXXVI, LXXXIX –148

       XCII. XCIV, XCV – 149

       XCVIII, XCIX – 150

       C, CII – 151

       CIV, CV – 152

CVI, CVII – 153
CVIII, CIX – 154
CXII, CXV, CXVII – 155
CXVIII, CXX – 156
CXXI, CXXIV – 157
CXXV, CXXVI – 158
CXXVIII, CXXXI, CXXXV – 159
CXXXVI – 160
CXXXVII, CXXXVIII – 161
CXLI, CLIV, CLV – 162
CLVII, CLXI – 163
CLXV, CLXVIII, CLXXII – 164
Chorale and Hymn – 166

Unpublished Work – 171
The Enigma – 173
Manifesto – 174
The Moon Is Number 18 – 175
Sphinx – 176
A Fantasy – 177
Post Mortum P.S. – 178
A Catalogue – 179
These Things – 180
In Particular – 181
Aphrodite – 183
On the Common – 184
O a Number I Kno – 185
Idyl – 186
Poem – 187
[Untitled] – 188
What Can I Tell You – 189
Il Saggio – 191
Sprout but Not Flower – 192
Ars Magna – 193
Tarot Diary – 201

Postscript – 249

When I say vortex
do I mean vertex as well.
I think not only of Wyndham Lewis & Pound
but of Jonas, Wieners, Marshall, Spicer & Blaser
Boston in the fifties of the 20th Century.
Remission does not advertise itself
but the old Boston vortex still swirls
thru the lives of us poets forever old forever young

Gerrit Lansing

Editorial Note

Even the shortest list of notable omissions from Donald Allen's groundbreaking anthology *The New American Poetry: 1945-1960* (Grove, 1960) would have to include Stephen Jonas (ca. 1921-1970). His absence is hardly surprising, however, if only because it would have been difficult in 1960 to obtain a comprehensive view of Jonas's work from the small number of poems scattered in little magazines of the period. The one single-author publication to his name at the time, *Love, the Poem, the Sea & Other Pieces Examined by Me* (White Rabbit Press, 1957), is a short long poem, four pages in the present edition, and Jonas's first substantial collection, *Transmutations* (Ferry Press), doesn't appear until 1966, from an English press at that.

But Jonas's significance to the extraordinary efflorescence of American poetry after the Second World War is beyond dispute. When he is taken into account, it's generally as a member of what is variously termed the "Occult School of Boston," the "Boston Renaissance," or some similar such phrase. This largely gay male configuration of poets has never achieved the notoriety of the San Francisco Renaissance, the New York School, or the Black Mountain Poets, in part because it overlaps with these groups. Broadly speaking, the Boston Renaissance is a mid-'50s phenomenon, beginning, say, when Jonas meets Edward Marshall in 1953. The galvanizing events of this group are the reading by Charles Olson at the Charles Street Meetinghouse in 1954—attended by Jonas, John Wieners, and Joe Dunn—and the temporary relocation to Boston of Jack Spicer and Robin Blaser in 1955-1956. Wieners and Dunn soon follow Olson to Black Mountain College but return while Spicer and Blaser are still in town. Olson himself—not a poet of the Boston Renaissance so much as its *éminence grise*—moves to nearby Gloucester, MA in 1956. This brief but intense period of ferment might be said to conclude in 1957, when Dunn moves to San Francisco and, at Spicer's behest, launches White Rabbit Press with Jonas's *Love, the Poem, the Sea & Other Pieces Examined by Me*, while back in Boston Wieners publishes the first issue of *Measure*.

Among this group, Wieners attests to the influence of Jonas, for example, in "Road of Straw," a section from one of his journals collected in *Stars Seen in Person: Selected Journals* (City Lights, 2015) (124-29). Jonas was also an inspiration to Spicer, particularly in terms of the serial poem. A solution to the problem posed by unfinishable modernist epics like Pound's *Cantos* or Olson's *Maximus Poems*, the serial poem was a major preoccupation for Jonas. His chief works in this regard are *Exercises for Ear* (Ferry Press, 1968) and the uncollected, unfinished series first written under the title *Orgasms*, and later, *Dominations*. He also began at least one further numbered but untitled series, individual examples of which appeared in magazines. On returning to San Francisco, Spicer immediately begins his first set of serial poems, *After Lorca*

(White Rabbit Press, 1957), the longest of which, "Ode to Walt Whitman," is dedicated to Jonas. Given the substantial increase in the reputations of Wieners and Spicer over the past several years, Jonas's reappearance in print is long overdue.

Nearly a quarter century has passed since the publication of the last major collection of Jonas's poetry, *Selected Poems* (Talisman House, 1994), edited with an introduction by Joseph Torra. This book remains the gold standard of Jonas scholarship, but it's no longer in print and secondhand copies have grown increasingly rare and expensive. The idea of preparing a new edition began a few years ago in conversation with Gerrit Lansing, who, along with Raffael De Gruttola, served as executor of Jonas's estate and custodian of his papers. Lansing, a significant American poet in his own right, moved to Gloucester in 1960, and became an important intimate of Olson, Wieners, and Jonas for the rest of their lives. Regrettably, Lansing passed away before this book achieved fruition, but we cannot overstate how instrumental to the realization of this project he was.

It is hoped that one day, some enterprising scholar/editor will undertake a complete reckoning of the work of Stephen Jonas. In creating *Arcana: A Stephen Jonas Reader*, we have had the more modest goal of simply bringing him back before the poetry-reading public. We do not claim to supersede the landmark achievement of *Selected Poems*. In large part because, concurrent with this edition, Bootstrap Press is publishing a standalone edition of *Exercises for Ear*, the entirety of which appears in *Selected Poems*, we have chosen not to reproduce the Talisman House book in favor of the "reader" format. We have, however, relied heavily on Joseph Torra's longstanding expertise on Jonas, reproducing many of the major poems whose texts Torra established in 1994. In particular, we have reproduced Torra's biographical "Introduction" to *Selected Poems*, as it would be almost impossible to improve upon. To conclude the book, we have added David Rich's extraordinary "Postscript," which provides an account of information concerning Jonas's deliberately self-obscured origins that has surfaced in the intervening years, mostly through Rich's own research.

As we have indicated above, many of the poems in *Arcana*, including the lengthy selection from *Exercises for Ear*, have been drawn from *Selected Poems*. We have also included a number of previously uncollected poems that were printed in little magazines, like *Yugen, Floating Bear, Origin*, and *Caterpillar*. To these we have added a short selection of previously unpublished poems from those papers of Jonas housed by Lansing and De Gruttola, if only to indicate that there remains more to fathom than what has already appeared. We have not attempted a chronological arrangement of the work, as Jonas frequently but by no means always dated his poems in MS. Instead, we have arranged the poems with an eye towards flow, as has been customary with editions of Jonas.

Finally, we have included a few items from Jonas' notebooks, 16 of which were in Lansing's possession at the time of his death. As David Rich notes in his "Postscript," Lansing directed Jonas to books on many esoteric subjects, and we have reproduced here his notes on alchemy ("Ars Magna") and the tarot ("Tarot Diary"). These notes are influenced by Raymond Lully's work on alchemy and works on the tarot by both Papus (Gerard Encausse) and Oswald Wirth, in addition to those titles Rich refers to. Jonas' "Tarot Diary" was of sufficient visual interest to warrant its reproduction *en face* with a transcription. These notebooks, along with the papers in Lansing's possession, will eventually be made available to scholarship once they are added to the Gerrit Lansing Papers at the Beinecke Rare Book and Manuscript Library at Yale University.

Arcana is dedicated to Gerrit Lansing and Raffael De Gruttola, keepers of the flame of Stephen Jonas.

Garrett Caples and Derek Fenner

Introduction

I

Americans imagine they can be anything they want to be. This is true of Stephen Jonas, the early part of whose history can only be conjectured. The closer one looks into his life before the mid-1940s, the muddier things get. What we know for certain begins with his discharge from the army. After this he drifted, spent time in New York, and then moved to Boston. Over the next two decades he lived a strained life that included run-ins with the law, a prison term, and mental breakdowns. But Stephen Jonas never lost touch with the idea of himself as a poet, or his commitment to writing. He remained the center of an evolving circle of Boston-area poets until his death in 1970.

Tracing Jonas's ancestry has proven futile. This is due in large part to his own efforts to erase certain aspects of his life and remain elusive about his past. His place and date of birth are unknown, though it has been reported that he was born somewhere in Georgia perhaps in 1920, 1925, or 1927. He was probably raised by adoptive parents and eventually changed his name (though never legally) from Rufus S. Jones to Stephen Jonas. Over the years he used a number of other aliases as well. At different times and to different people, Jonas offered different versions of his early years.

Poet David Rattray in his memoir "Lightning Over the Treasury" in *How I Became One of the Invisible* writes that Jonas "was born a mulatto in post-World War One rural Georgia, a world where lynching and fiery crosses and gunshots fired from passing cars in the night were commonplace." Rattray also relates a tale Jonas told of being seduced by a female teacher in Georgia, with a terrified Jonas running home naked through the fields. All of this appears unlikely, especially in light of a letter from Jonas to his friend Raffael De Gruttola:

> what you say abt my latin blood is correct. i was adopted by The
> Friends at abt age three. my own parents, i didn't know (my mother
> Perreira and father Santos) i was taken by them (my adoptive
> parents) to Rockland County New York, where I grew up. My
> adopted father was Scotch-Dutch Kirkland, his mother & Jonas his
> father. my adopted mother was Dayhoff & dont remember what
> her mother's family name was. they were both "American"—sense
> of Henry James. i have been to New Bedford where I was born,
> but think it a horror. as far as i can make out, my mother was
> Spanish—(i think Creole i.e. French-Spanish) her mother's people
> settled in San Juan & later, i suppose to New Bedford where she met
> & married my father who was Portuguese—what else, i donno. he
> was a fisherman & later sailor. my adopted father had some business

interests in New Bedford & Boston—fishing sloops i think—so must have known my father through this association. all of which qualifies me to be a "grease ball" par excellence.

Of course, this elaborate tracing of Jonas's roots may be a fabrication. What is clear is that he repeatedly attempted to keep people guessing. To those who knew him in his Boston years, Jonas was a generous and compassionate friend. People were always welcome in his various apartments. "If I'm not home, come in through the window, everybody does." Once he pulled in a tree limb so that it grew through an open window. If the children of his junkie friends were hungry, he fed them. He liked to cook, and it's common to find recipes next to reading lists in his notebooks. Jonas was extremely resourceful, one time re-wiring the electricity in an apartment building so he received his power free from his landlord's circuit. Some of his food came from late-night foraging of produce dumpsters at the public market. To his writer and artist friends, he was a major source of information and inspiration.

Jonas often passed as Hispanic or Portuguese and didn't feel comfortable when someone referred to him as black. But in some ways, he liked his "blackness" and the fact that he could travel in circles not immediately open to whites. His associations and friendships were nearly always with whites, but in black and white worlds, he was an outsider—a rootless, social renegade, which at times created in him an insecurity and self-doubt that he struggled with throughout his life. It seems unlikely that he ever came to terms with his racial identity. While in the eyes of society he was subversive, and though he aligned himself closer to Malcolm X than to Martin Luther King, he was neither of the political left nor the right.

The open, widespread movement driven by Black pride and civil rights consciousness was barely under way in the 1950s. By comparison, notions of gay pride were embryonic. That Jonas was a homosexual further estranged him from the mainstream. Long-term gay relationships evaded him. He often fell in love with straight white men, or druggies or runaways he befriended, who cared for him but rarely reciprocated with the kind of love Jonas offered. Asides, references, and dedications to these relationships and lovers are abundant in his poems.

Jonas survived largely on a monthly military disability check, a pension he told some friends he'd rigged while working in the army's records division. The money allowed him to live simply but well enough to pursue his range of interests full time. His Boston circle of friends and acquaintances included poets, artists, musicians, prostitutes, runaways, junkies, and thieves. In this underground environment he found sustenance for his life and poetry. Jonas's tuning in to the street life and its inhabitants became an essential source of material for his writing. His keen ear enabled him to transcribe the language and various voices he heard and get them down in the poems.

Jonas's poetry became a record of his investigations, a system of mapping out his examinations. He had a great passion for music, a fascination with economics, and a genuine interest in history, mythology, philosophy, science, the arts, magic, alchemy, and politics. His interest in poetry led him to Cid Corman's West End Library poetry group where in 1948 and 1949 he read the work of Pound, Williams, and later Olson and Creeley. Jonas was primarily self-taught; his notebooks are full of extensive reading/listening lists and treatises on his discoveries. (He stole many of his books and records from the Boston Public Library.) Jonas did a good deal of his preliminary writing in his notebooks, which he tended daily. These are full of his far-reaching investigations and drafts of what would become his finished poems. Though Jonas never formalized a poetics, his system was in effect a process of finding out.

II

By 1954 Jonas was a disciplined, practicing writer. In the fall of that year at Charles Olson's Charles Street Meeting House reading (a reading that transformed the non-academic Boston poetry scene), John Wieners introduced the young poet Joe Dunn to Stephen Jonas. After the reading, Dunn, his wife Carolyn, Wieners, and Jonas talked through the night. Dunn reports that Jonas was "a fountain of books and information." Jonas constantly gave out lists of books to read; he had steeped himself in the work of Pound and Williams, as well as contemporary poets like Creeley and Olson. This was an eye-opener for Dunn and Wieners, whose college readings in modern poetry had only exposed them to Eliot. It was the Olson reading and Jonas's ensuing encouragement that led Wieners and Dunn to Black Mountain College in North Carolina. The two tried to get Jonas to follow, but he preferred to remain in Boston, a city he had grown to love.

When Black Mountain College was in the process of closing down, Dunn and Wieners returned to Boston. There they met Jack Spicer and Robin Blaser who had moved to Boston in 1955. Blaser was working at Harvard's Widener Library, and he had found Spicer a job at the rare book room at the Boston Public Library. Spicer was slow to respond to the likes of Dunn, Wieners, and Jonas. He despised Boston and didn't believe anyone there could be writing viable poetry. Through Dunn's insistence, Spicer read the work of Jonas and Wieners and was astonished. Lewis Ellingham and Kevin Killian, in their biography of Jack Spicer, write, "What drew Spicer to Jonas? One reason is surely Spicer's curiosity about Black Mountain College. Despite Spicer's tumultuous relationship to Olson's poetics, he was drawn intellectually to the coherence of his system, and the young poets of Boston were pure products of that thinking.... Uniformly charming, witty, lovable, they sought poetry by a systematic derangement of the senses, a system which left little time or inclination for ordinary jobs or schedules. The most liminal of all was Jonas...." Blaser reports that he and Spicer were amazed at the range of subject matter Jonas was already folding into his work.

Joe Dunn has described the summer of 1956 as "that intense summer." Jonas, Wieners, Dunn, Spicer, and Blaser were all living within blocks of each other on the inexpensive backside of Beacon Hill. Meeting regularly, writing, and sharing their work, the group began publishing a Boston "Newsletter," which they sent off to friends. According to Ellingham and Killian:

> This odd document, a curious blend of acid raillery and low
> camp, features "Coming Attractions" such as Jonas' "Cock Drill,"
> an obvious pun on Pound's then-new "Rock Drill" section of the
> Cantos, as well as Wieners' "Wieners." The newsletter came with
> instructions: *Post whatever pages of it poke you in the eye in the most public place*
> *you can find—i.e., an art gallery, a bohemian bar, or a lavatory frequented by poets.*
> It's a very gay text, and its emphasis on collaboration, disjunction,
> gender politics, "nonsense" locates it at the exact site of post-
> modern practice. It was received with delight by Robert Duncan
> during the last faltering days of Black Mountain College.

What has been called the "Boston Renaissance" was merely a handful of poets who got to know each other one summer. But the "Boston Gang," as Spicer called them, participated in establishing an alternative poetry scene in Boston that shared an affinity with Black Mountain, Beat, New York, and San Francisco "schools." In September the group gave a public reading. Disgusted by the fact that only eight people showed up, Spicer planned his return to the West Coast. But the group's summer encounter was fruitful. After hearing a Bird recording coming from Joe and Carolyn Dunn's apartment, Spicer wrote "Song for Bird and Myself," which would be his transitional poem. The same summer Jonas wrote "Love, the Poem, the Sea & Other Pieces Examined by Me," a pivotal poem for him.

This was Jonas's first important poem, bringing together the essential elements of his work within a system that could contain them. His method is poetry as examination, entwining polymorphic themes through a projective-like musical delineation. The poems reflect Jonas's sense of the classics, history, American culture, music (especially jazz), the language and life of the streets, love found and lost. Beginning with "Love, the Poem, the Sea & Other Pieces Examined by Me," it became regular practice for Jonas to consciously address *the poem at hand* while in the middle of writing it, a charting of the poem as a thinking/breathing entity. When Joe Dunn moved to San Francisco in 1957, he carried the manuscript of Jonas's "Love, the Poem, the Sea & Other Pieces Examined by Me" with him. It became the first publication of his White Rabbit Press.

Though Jack Spicer's stay in Boston was brief (he left Boston in November 1956), his artistic relationship with Jonas must be underscored. In many ways they were at opposite ends in terms of their poetics, but each greatly inspired the other. They shared common social and cultural interests, and each was vehemently skeptical about much of the poetry being written and published at the time, especially the more formal poetry associated with the New Criticism. Ellingham and Killian write that it was Jonas who taught Spicer "to use anger (as opposed to angry irony) in a poem":

> In a sense, Jonas was the objective correlative of Spicer's longings and fears, the outsider complete. He'd even changed his name to redefine the new self he'd created, like a butterfly emerging from a cocoon. Born plain "Jones," *Jonas* perhaps better reflects all kinds of antimonies—the man in the belly of the great beast, the man chosen by God, the sufferer, the exile. Spicer (who played with the closeness of his own name to "Spider," and who abjured the use of the formal "John Lester Spicer" in favor of the folksy "Jack") was a firm believer in notional power.

When Spicer translated Lorca's "Ode to Walt Whitman" in his book *After Lorca*, he dedicated it to Jonas. And in his detective novel, *The Tower of Babel*, he based his "Washington Jones" character on Jonas. Jonas responded with numerous poems dedicated and addressed to Spicer, including major poems like "Canto Jondo for Soul Brother Jack Spicer, His Beloved California & Andalusia of Lorca," and "Morphogenesis, (being a conventionalization of 'Morphemes' of Jack Spicer)." Jonas often refers to fellow poets in his writings, but Spicer is omnipresent.

In 1957 John Wieners edited and published the first of three issues of the magazine *Measure*. This first issue included Charles Olson, Edward Marshall, Ed Dorn, Larry Eigner, Fielding Dawson, Frank O'Hara, Robin Blaser, Jack Spicer, Jonathan Williams, and Robert Duncan. At the center of the issue was Stephen Jonas's manifesto-like "Word on Measure." *Measure* nurtured the small but lively Boston group, and it was their lifeline to the poetry activity in New York and San Francisco. At this time Jonas hit his stride and wrote profusely. He was regularly writing shorter, lyric pieces and had already written several significant long poems, including "Love, the Poem..." and "Word on Measure." It was not uncommon, after a two- or three-day period, for Jonas to appear with a twenty- or thirty-page draft.

Wherever Jonas lived in Boston, his apartment was inevitably a kind of nexus for various underworld activities. Although Jonas was never a junkie himself, junkies, prostitutes, thieves, and runaways were common house guests who might drop by to crash for the night, shoot up and stash their drugs or loot. At some point during 1957 and 1958, Jonas and some of his associates became involved in scamming record and book clubs. Addressed to C. H. Corman and Dr. Charles Duncan among others, books and records were ordered and mailed to Jonas's apartment. These were then sold with the money going to purchase drugs.

In September of 1958, Jonas was arrested and held for a month at Suffolk County prison before being tried on forty-seven counts of mail fraud. He chose to defend himself, and he reportedly told the judge that in a country of grand larceny, petty larceny was no crime. He was convicted and sentenced to prison for six months, of which he served four in the federal penitentiary in Danbury, Connecticut. Apparently, Jonas immensely enjoyed his jail experience—meeting other gay men and mob-types, and identifying with his hero Ezra Pound's incarceration. When the authorities refused him paper, Jonas wrote on toilet paper. Naturally, his prison experiences and the voices of inmates appeared in his future writings.

Upon his release from prison and return to Boston in 1959, a newer group of poets began to make up the Jonas circle. Jonas generated much interest in poetry among younger friends, reading and critiquing their works, always pushing the idea of the poem as more than self-expression. To younger writers like Dale Landers and Tony Sherrod, Jonas became a mentor. He also became emotionally involved with these men to varying degrees and in 1961 wrote several long poems, including "A Poem for Dale Landers" and "A Trio for Tony Sherrod," in which he raised all these issues. Alas, Sherrod and Landers eventually left Boston, Landers dying of an overdose in Mexico City.

These were highly charged times. Many of Jonas's associates used heroin, speed, and alcohol. But poetry remained a constant. Around 1960 Jonas met Gerrit Lansing, and they became lifelong friends. They shared mutual interests in gay life, music, poetry, the arts, and the occult. In the early 1960s they saw each other in Boston or New York, to which Jonas made occasional trips. Lansing crashed at Jonas's apartment when passing through Boston, and he eventually settled in Gloucester where he edited SET, a magazine that published Jonas, Olson, LeRoi Jones, Diane Wakoski, Robert Kelly, John Wieners, Ed Dorn, and others. Lansing and Jonas continued to correspond and visit, sharing their poetry, reading lists, discoveries, and gossip until Jonas's death.

Mental breakdowns had left Jonas hospitalized in the past. At one point in the early 1960s, he walked out of a hospital unit and got to New York where he was acting so wild that even close friends feared him. He was hearing voices through his teeth and fillings. Later, this experience fueled "Orgasm VII: *The Oracle Bone*." There were times in his life when Jonas experienced states of paranoia, yet at other times he was capable of great clarity and insight. He often took psychotropic medication prescribed by doctors in combination with street drugs. He was especially fond of speed, and heavy doses of it may have contributed to his bouts of paranoia. Several times Jonas was hospitalized, stabilized, and eventually released.

During the early 1960s Jonas stepped up work on a series of long poems called *Orgasms*. Left incomplete, these are his most ambitious writing project. Although clearly in debt to Pound's *Cantos* and, to a lesser degree, Olson's *Maximus Poems*, Jonas had no grand design in mind. These were bursts of his enormous energy and intellect, reflecting his encyclopedic mind. The subject matter of an *Orgasm* might range from street incidents to the classics, from the Tarot to the Constitution, from the voice of a prison inmate to a quote from Thomas Jefferson. There's an improvisational quality Jonas had learned from years of listening to jazz. The poems are a collage addressing the breadth of Jonas's investigations. Shifting in tone and focus from line to line, here fragmented structure becomes a mirror of the actual life-psyche driving the writing.

In June 1962 Jonas wrote to Lansing that "the whole picture of the *Great Work* is clear." However, Jonas's view of the *Orgasms* continually shifted. By 1967 he had written about forty pieces and in a letter to Lansing stated, "there are 15 or so *Orgasms* that I don't intend on using—but shall salvage them as the Light moves me to it." At the time of his death he'd even decided to change the name of the project to *Dominations*. Most of the poems that survive in manuscript are titled *Orgasms* (and were published as such), but it is apparent that had Jonas lived longer, he would have retitled them. So for this selection I have chosen to title them *Orgasms/Dominations*. It's apparent from the surviving manuscripts that Jonas changed numbers as time went on, and he continued to write new installments causing some confusion. In May 1967 he wrote to Lansing:

> i've written two sets of XX series/?! i can't explain why for i don't understand it myself. when I wrote the *Orgasms* (JFK-Banker series) last summer, i was well aware that there was a XX series already written, but i did it again! but i allow the, what i term "poetic judgment", take precedent over my formal judgment—i follow the former. but to date the "poetic judgment" has not directed me as to what numbers to give the prior XX series. well, we shall see.

The *Orgasms* in the first "XX" series, which were written before the abovementioned "JFK-Banker Series," may have become the *Orgasms* that comprise the "Second Series."

Each time Jonas moved into new territory with a series of *Orgasms*, his own sense of the project changed. There are threads of correspondences throughout the series, and new themes emerge from time to time. This is most evident in the "JFK-Banker Series" from 1966 and 1967. These are electrifying political rants, Jonas up on the soapbox spewing forth his most didactic and anti-Semitic writing. Picking up on Pound's economic and historical perspective ("what keeps me sane in this madhouse of a country, is that I have read & digested a few of Pound's indicated areas of economics & history"), Jonas maps out a case of government conspiracy through an exploration of the National Banking Act of 1862 and the Federal Reserve Act of 1913. His heroes are Sam Adams, Thomas Jefferson, Andrew Jackson, Abraham Lincoln, and John F. Kennedy, and he cites the Lincoln and Kennedy assassinations as examples of a nation undermined by foreign-influenced usury—i.e., usury that Jonas believed was Jewish in origin. These poems are angry, dogmatic treatises that can become tiresome, repetitive, ugly, and hateful.

IV

Jonas is one of the great jazz voices in American poetry; he wrote with an improviser's sensibility. His spontaneity, starts, stops, inflections are unique. He adopted Williams's revolution of the line and tuned an idiom to his own jazz-ear. He frequently read poetry out loud, including Pound, over jazz. His letters and notebooks are filled with music-related references. Lester Young, Billie Holiday, Charlie Parker, Coleman Hawkins, Ornette Coleman, and others (including classical composers) make their way into the poems as subject matter and into the underlying formal structure. In a letter to Raffael De Gruttola, Jonas lists the music he would listen to on a typical day:

> Scott & I got some new sides: Vivaldi, Bach, Rameau, (couldn't find any Francesco da Milano!!) Scarlatti, Corelli, & of course Mozart also Pergolesi—Concerto No. 2, 3, 4 & Concerto for Flute & Strings which Scott tried to wrangle out of me by offering to trade a "pres" side WHICH I GAVE HIM. Got a Carmen McRae, Modern Jazz Quartet—*The Sheriff* & a new Frank (eternal) Sinatra yeahhh...

Jonas always impressed younger poets with the fact that poetry was music first, not simply a matter of trying to say something. And he often lamented that the younger writers didn't listen. In his poems Jonas sacrificed anything to get the music right. Content, meaning, and spelling all came after the fact. In 1961 he wrote to Cid Corman:

Knollledge and the *mot juste* just aint my forte. You had better realize
now once and for all that me and "the correct way" just don't
make it. When I write, I write listening for the sound of the word
and I come as close to the spelling of it as spelling will permit me.
Usually that is not close enuf. What I'm trying here to get over to
you Cid is that I am a Poet (I hope so) drunk with the music of
langwidge. Hell, man its all I can do to get the sounds down let-
alone wrassle with a fucking dictionary.

As spontaneous as Jonas's poems are, it's clear from his notebooks and the
number of drafts some poems went through, that there was a tremendous
amount of revision in his process. He worked his line to make music. Citing
his mentors in a letter to Gerrit Lansing, Jonas wrote, "Pound and WCW
constantly revised and reformed their line. The earlier and by comparison
their later things reveal some change in speech rhythms." In the same letter
Jonas discussed how he'd spent weeks on a poem, trying to get the metrics of
it right. Free verse, he explained, could have "dire consequences. If we speak
in Time then our things must arrest and retain this time. I have tried (short
of counting) to recognize in the Ear such measures as are contain'd in speech
especially 'charged speech' that as it were laboring to bring forth, newly born,
some particular, worth of celebrating..."

By 1965 Jonas's reputation among other poets had grown. His poems
appeared in many little magazines including *Yugen*, *Floating Bear*, and *Origin*, and
editors solicited his work. But a full-length book still eluded him. In July
of that year he received a fan latter. An Englishman named Andrew Crozier,
who was at the State University of New York at Buffalo, wrote saying he'd
read Jonas's poems in various magazines and asked if Jonas would let him
publish a collection of his poems. The collection would be small since funds
were limited. This must have posed a problem for Jonas, whose body of work
could have filled several volumes. Nonetheless, in March 1966 Crozier's Ferry
Press in London brought out Jonas's first substantial volume, *Transmutations* (the
alchemical term for transforming base metals into gold), with an introduction
by John Wieners and cover drawings by Basil King. It contained an impressive
selection of Jonas's various long and short poems, including several *Orgasms*,
and short poems called *Exercises for Ear*.

Working from older poems, notebook drafts, and new compositions, Jonas
had been honing his short takes down to quick, lively riffs he titled *Exercises for
Ear*. In these poems, Jonas knew that he'd hit on something essential. "(Pres is
still the genius for understatement)," he wrote to Raffael De Gruttola:

> What I'm getting at can only be gotten at (effectively) in the short
> poem. a little chune that is complete from the first word of it to

the last....I would venture to say that WCW hit on this clean classic stance (as clean & as classic as Pisanello or Botticelli are clearly defined w/o clutter of excessive descriptive—(adjectives) etc from a study of D.H. Lawrence. However, most of D.H. Lawrence (to my ear) is not successful or "are not" I shd. say, Poem-chunes. but he does these aforementioned "musts". Lawrence (exception *Ship of Death*) never mastered free verse form. Pound describes this quality in WCW as "opacity". I incorporated this quality of WCW also in my short poems.

Jonas adopted the encyclopedic, fragmented structure of Pound's *Cantos* in his *Orgasms*. In the *Exercises for Ear*, Jonas took his cue from Williams's spare, direct, down-to-earth sensibility. In the *Exercises* his great multiplicity of references remain, but the brevity of the pieces doesn't allow them to become convoluted by the barrage, as they can in some of the *Orgasms/Dominations*.

The *Exercises for Ear* swing. Their polyphony and rhythmic textures shift in intensity, pitch, and timbre. In some poems Jonas uses direct statement, in others pure image. There's a condensed drama and an immediacy of the streets' rhythms, voices, and commonplace occurrences. "Ear is brain," Gerrit Lansing writes in his introduction to the Ferry Press edition of *Exercises for Ear*. The poems are gritty, freewheeling but controlled. Jonas's line is as tight or as fluid as it needs to be. Each poem is individually spring-loaded, laden with riffs, starts and stops. In terms of his shorter poems, the *Exercises for Ear* are the apex of Jonas's efforts. Jonas spent much time meticulously tending poems in *Exercises for Ear* until they'd reached their musical potential. He labored over the change of a word or the deletion of a comma—the musical composition his primary concern. Referring to the poems in a letter, he wrote, "they're swinging & let's hope once & for all the 'jazz poetry' hassle be resolved. The methodology is in the language that hugs the scene like Zukofsky's vowels to necks of consonants." The 174 poems that make up the *Exercises for Ear* never lose the tune. Written at the height of his creative powers, the book remains a seminal work of American poetry in a jazz idiom, the only complete book of a single work or series that Jonas would collect and see into publication.

V

Jonas remained active and befriended another group of younger writers including Raffael De Gruttola (to whom he dedicated the *Exercises*). On Saturday nights Jonas held Magic Evenings at his Beacon Hill apartment. Locals attended, as did those visiting from out-of-town such as Robert Kelly and Harvey Brown. They listened to music and read poetry, and discussions snowballed. At the time Jonas was attempting to organize the *Orgasms/Dominations* into some kind of order that would make publishing sense, and he was also writing new poems, including another series of short poems to which he gave Roman numerals but never titled. The series remains uncollected.

Jonas was also slowing down. He'd grown indifferent to relationships, having soured on sex and love. He encountered long periods where he couldn't write. His physical health began to fail, the intensity with which he'd lived catching up. His teeth were rotting, and he'd lost the vitality of his looks. Near the end of his life he faced deepening bouts of depression. While moving things into his last apartment on Anderson Street with some friends, he became short of breath and would have collapsed without their aid. Apparently he was still taking street drugs in various combinations as well as prescribed medications.

Describing Jonas's face in his memoir "Lightning Over The Treasury," David Rattray could also be describing Jonas's poetry: "disquietingly vivid and mobile; it could move, as I later discovered to my increasing consternation, through a succession of masks reflecting hilarity, sympathetic interest, disdain, indignation, murderous rage, or screaming terror, all with an intensity and speed that very few could keep up with, since many of these masks were outward signs of the chemical upheaval with which his body and mind were continually afflicted." It is this *succession of masks* that comes to mind when I consider Jonas and his poetry. His was a system of upheaval, the continuous turning over of matter and the transmutation of that process into poetry.

On the tenth of February 1970, Jonas, who had been devastated by Olson's death one month earlier (and Spicer's death in 1965), died alone in his Anderson Street apartment. His death certificate reports his color as white, lists the cause of death as an overdose of Doriden, his parents unknown, and his place of birth simply "Georgia." Nebulous as the details of his background are, Stephen Jonas's poems remain a poet's faith in the audible, palpable energy of the imagination. With this selection some old Boston corridors are no longer silent. *Listen.*

Joseph Torra
Boston, 1994

This introduction originally appeared in Selected Poems *by Stephen Jonas, ed. Joseph Torra* (*Talisman House,* 1994).

PUBLISHED POEMS

INVOCATION

O generation gone
    thoroughly to seed
yr. legislators, yr. heads
    of state
            a great informal
racket without in-
        struction in-
capable of re-
    capitulation & no
distinction between
      subject & object
suffices anymore
to distinguish time &
    place
Long gaps appear in the
    contours of the language
(as tho' a mere pencil could
      indicate so much grief)
A language whose word
    of true meaning has been
      severely lost.

      envoi
O lady carved in rosewood
    or set in alabaster
    I pray you
      make us again
the tall grasses
  to bend & part
before your footfall.
Teach us to sin
    and not to sin.

. . . . . AN EAR INJURED BY HEARING THINGS
(after a statement of Jack Spicer's)

thoughts march
across the page
orderly
the mind
hems & haws
de-
    fining the line a
metrical dance
not, I caution you
preconceived
free? only
the mind
violating
the law taking
exceptions to
create (never to
new laws (oh, no a
flexibility
it seeks
(tender vineshoots
from the old year's
vine stock(s)
ten-
      tacles up
the wall feelers out to
the new ways
design?
an arrangement
of parts
mere-
      ly particulars
of the Poem
traced (for the mind
sketches
technique?
long since
burrowd under
but the pattern
's obvious as are

markings on bird
form? yes
what else
looming before you
underbrush
cleard that the spaces show
clean thru
to a finished what
have you.

Spring 1961

THE OUTRAGED GENIUS

hopped-up
      & juiced
    you must have
        a tune in yr head
(—staggers for the door
        bounding into
        chairs
            other
                  patrons pur-
      sued of their
               abandond
                        laughter
        protestations of those
    he missed
—allow me
        come i'll be yr Virgil
& together we'll get said
        what must be
buggin' you
      we'll start tonite
say an epic for starter
       —a few of yr
         choice lyrics
            for chaser
posterity will be at yr heels
        (what'-R-yu
          sum kinna-nut?

1962

BLACKSTONE PARK
(Dans le vieux parc solitaire et glacé)

in this park of dilapidated times
            where no one comes save
                        the bums & those
who love beneath the vine or the rose

winos toss empty pints
            on-to the half shell of
a no longer running fount
dry voices of castrated hopes

complain to a jagged moon
                        in its final resolve
at the last bench of a row
            two shadows equivocate

they have no sex nor time
their words are witherd grasses
            beneath the shuddering night;
some old ecstasy performed for fools

who believe the words they've said
                        when the wind is down
and the green innocence of death
            stalks the place

with a rattle of two elevated cars
            overhead   hang-dog
and headed for the suburbs

1966

SUBWAY HAIKU

everytime the president speaks
i close my mouth
thinking i talk too much
& there are voices underneath you
old mr. giacconetti cleaning his pipes
they'll shut you up if you let 'em

          so i move around
          & dont sit in one place too long

     everytime i close my eyes
     a new office building goes up
     startling me into taking a pill

           60 words per/min
           the ad for typist sd

/never thought i'd make it up the stairs
the last words i heard June say

         3 needles
         & in both sides
         they give me
         & all for getting
         a sick cock

     joe joe joe
     dont eat crow

      & my box dont work
      a spring broke that
      triggers the mechanism
          underneath

    speed king
    the washing machine sd
    in red underneath chrome

         o my tenderette
         wrapped in tin foil
         from a bottom
         that slides out

dont get mononucleosis
it takes a year to cure
      kissing sickness

                i tell you the sentence is doomed

                        dont take the trains
                        ride the verb into town
                        take a local
                        w/more nouns to stop at

            tonite i want a full moon
            like a slice of provolone
            where rats nibbled at the edge

it costs too much
to have an opinion

              o joy i lost yr bread
              in a crap game
                    & made you sad

                      o my head where things
                      are all screwed up

          even in my dreams
          creditors chase me thru
          a fantastic landscape on mars
          so i hide my poetry
          under an assumd name

                    winos looking at me
                    with dimes & nickels for eyes

              o eastman kodak people
              w/yr shades drawn

     lover rush into my arms
     186,000 m per/sec

             people lining up to see
             la dolce vita sd the movie marquee

o mechanical bird singing one song
you are yesterdays late edition
lying in the gutter

          philologists searching for unicorns
                  in out of space

o ed marshall w/yr soapbox
by united farmers

             old rugged cross just played out
             on a jukebox by
             universal parts inc.

        o jeffersonian 3 ring circus
        m.c.'d by hamiltonians
             w/trained & performing press

castro hates chicken
& wont be tempted

            by big money
            seeding latin american
            counter revolutionary clouds

        tv's getting cheaper than ever
        there's mass production for you

and this day just just slid down
behind the manual arts school

                  o droopin penis
                  my cocatrice
                  what queen of the night
                  makes you drip

flowers opend and light waiting
&
   bees too busy to bother
              anymore

christian song playd out
but the mechanism wont reject
                        sacrifice space
                        to yr dead gods

        scared yes i'm scared
        everytime i pick a knife up
        i see yr face in a late edition

old woman w/yr teeth gone
& not much left to chew on

                o pie for all yr crustiness
                you dont move me

                                use words sparingly
                                so few of us left

o gasman you took my meter out

                o lonely world
                with yr/ penis out
                to fuck up the universe

                write
                        i must write & keep on writing
                        till my ink's run out

                music
                a form of speech a
                        conversational racket with
                        some time a
                                yak-a-T-yak means
                        of talking back

1962

THE CELIBATE

my ole uncle so & so
      (now w/God) had
(among other things I
      hesitate to touch upon—)
the (so help me God) biggest
    piece ('Scuse the Xpression) in
the town athletic (unmaled)
assoc. Christ! he was al-
      ways (between workouts w/bar-
bells & the like) beating it (and
   at the mirror yet) outsized (and
   no exaggeration) down to
his knees
       what can I tell you
he was (a boy I played w/it
   in bed) hung (my hand ta' god) like
   a horse & could have
(had he turnd pro & stopd
      playin' w/hisself) kept
ole Christian Science ladies
   (w/fat dividend checks
from husbands mostly dead) happy

BRISK WALK TO PAVILION OF GOOD CROPS & PEACE
(Three Versions from the Chinese)

Trees all got up & deck'd out
   w/ flowers in their hair
      hillocks
like crisp new money;
     sun about to split
a scene laying out
     the green carpet to an
infinity of unconcern'd that cld
      care less
        as these

here today gone tomorrows
    tramp up & down fronting
the pavilion
& the flowers
    underfoot

     Ou Yang Hsiu (1007-1072) Sung Dynasty

Trees horny w/ leaves
    scratching their crotches
full of bird tweet
     as the hard-on hills
get a blow-job from the east
all to censor'd bird songs
   & the flower orgie.
when this wino
   comes out of his stupor
it will be too late for
     spring

     Ou Yang Hsiu (1007-1072) Sung Dynasty

ON THE ESPLANADE

as snow flying past
   on the picture tube
& petals of ten thousand springs
    carried by the wind
blowing no good

then the fade-out
      & I turn to drink.
Pair of kingfishers shack up in
      the pavilion with rotten teeth
stoned bi-sexual unicorns
      case the park &
the thud-like empty tomb
      (to each his own
          after his kind or a folded
             quilt)
to think I let an underpaid
      pencil pushing bureaucratic
        appointment deter me
from a here she goes fire one
      (just ripe for making)
        plum blossoms

Tu Fu (713-770) T'ang Dynasty

GREEN

    as the day
you were born
without leaves with-
             out
    stripped
        barely
   distinguishable
from other heathen
          branches
baptised by understanding
    the overfalling
             showers falling
affectionately upon birches
      boughs of
old family trees are
   sentimental
attachments to
      roots joined in
soil swollen clusters
    of sublimation like
lines hidden
       never washed
publicly but
     bathed rumors
in clothes closets
       behind doors of
  juries
    locked in
to keep out
    the public-like
        rain
   endlessly falling
in January when hell
  even the yellow
   is an orange
   hidden in trees
bathed in smog soaked
     landscape
endlessly falling
   and rising.

TENSONE WITH RELENT

My things
        it is high time we put on
a disreputable face
            & circulated
        out among that unmanageable din
          of verse makers
let us speak in stricture of
            terza rima
concerning their un-
          metrical skills
Let us recite at them in
           outrageous meters
Oh to hell with them & really, you know
nothing will ever come of all this
a barking dog seldom bites
and anyway above them slowly
        if you want to feel this with me
moves the slow waters of the Styx
and we know their voices will
          ultimately drown
in heavy odors of pig fat, besides.

THREE DANCE MOODS FOR EAR

                i

The smile that curved so
                once about the lips
                lifted at the corners
and yawnd into the spaces left for words
        that never come
                or hides, like the subtle ivy,
its tentacles beneath a green shade,
                looking out,
solicits no applause.

                ii

. . . nor, in this common light, have we
                fared better, most
                        unhappy lot
                made no-
                        toriously reasonable;
chance and circumstance/turns all to
                cold metallic purpose
                setting no sights to move or to dance
the image. Dismantled
                all that machinery
                                departed.
Leaving the scene/to,
                maudlin abstractions,
                passions too powerful to be believed
or if believed,
                too long endured.

                iii

In the age of frescoes he
                married the classic image
adding to/it his own
                        outraged agonies
                depending from the lower limb
                        of some Paduan master,
the vulture surveys almost the entire can-

45

vas. So one thinks of
          Chagall's husband floating past,
Caught-
      up in a swirl
           of past regrets. It is
an audacious willingness to experience.

November, 1961

46

THE RETURN

Remembering
            it is returning
somehow to the familiar.
            In the interval
there has been a loss.
                  Alone
one suffers it.
                  Alone
—with his thoughts
            locked out,
the old man is
            with us no longer.
  Impotent
            what else is there for him
unless in old age he write it.
The birth of tragedy
                        remembered it is
all remembered
                  Unconscious the sea surge
will not let him forget
                  save death intercedes
putting an end to all tragedy.

from ORGASMS/DOMINATIONS

I

In the end.
   It is sd.
      men improve on what they know
          they do know.
     In the eleventh book of the Odyssey
             they know
     there is no satisfaction in death.
The child of Praxiteles
      reaching for some object
           (undisclosed)
    now lost,
      once held in the right hand of Hermes.
To replace something
     where, formerly, there was something
          is something.

    (. . . how do you write a poem?
    (you don't unless you think
    of a wheel) (huh?) (i mean you don't
    it comes to you) o you mean (o
    i don't know what i mean look
    you're buggin' me like man
    —do you mind . . . ?
)
        It is
         an honest question
             as such
    deserves an honest answer
        (yah,
         later)
In relation to the body,
     the head small
       (still Praxiteles);
The universe is not limited
      by space. Its vastness
     should not prove a deception,
         within
    the mind's confines
      embracing
       more than that vastness. Reach

approximations
                        previously reached. In due course
one comes
            to his destination
                            approximated.
It is not enough today
                to say
            "write"
        —looking into the heart of light—
                                but then
                (. . . what do you think people are to think
                seeing you come up with
                                —those fantastic lines
                biting into the white paper . . . see what I mean
                that sets it off but where-to is anybody's guess
                . . . venus, mars, the kitchen sink, south station where
                you were going to meet that queen with the
                        gone stick . . .)

                        these are illumination
                                        problems
            playing upon a surface
                                profound or other, and,
                        short of our time, have been
            workd successfully out
                                in stone, upon canvas
                                        and other media.
The depressed areas
                causing shadows,
                            should detain no one. Here,
            relief should be thought
                                —as the palette knife
            is not applicable—
                        of the Word. Here,
I am myself,
            intimately,
                    concerned.
                        Thought examining processes
                (the which I have,
                                myself, submitted) lead
            onto the gridiron
                        of Carcassone. Ordered,
                                the mind
            quick to discern order,

49

                          is not itself ordered.

The reverse,

                not necessarily verse,

                         would be

                                a play of reversals. The Play,

which should be Verse,

                    is no more than a game

                                of chance-audience

                  participating to hurl

                            their emotions, like so many balls

                  across a pro-

                      scenium

                        as though there were no such thing as

                re-

                    ality

. . . such were the impositions I suffered—

                          mask in hand,

                              to the wings, I beat

                            my retreat.

This is the way with the mind—

                      re-creation of

                          its own handiwork;

                saying behind the mask:

                          "I am the way

                  I am the light."

Who would believe it would believe

                      a lie of eternal contrivance—

tale twice-told by an idiot-fool,

                    himself blinded by folly,

                short of stepping onto

                          a yawning precipice.

From a mountain trip,

                  down a winding path, I found it difficult

                  to breathe

                      in the lower air.

                Where else could I find

                        concern for my own concern

                now I ask myself

                    now that I am

                          knee-deep

                in the thick of it. Leave?

Thinking: a change of place,

                taking to that place in the head

                the old place:

what you depart from . . .

is also

where you have

come to.

About myself

about what I find out

about the Poem & in it:

Like Oedipus,

but with less, Oh in-

finitely less

violence

—take out my sights

not so much to contrition

as to examine the image

they have made me out

To Begin With

II

(Moon, 1st phase
is risen)

There is

in that place

"In quella parte

dove sta memoria

Prende suo stato" . . .

some consolation

We speak of it

sometimes

when we are tired

—just plain

weary of it

—all.

. . . oh nothin' in par-

tic-u-lar its just

ev'-

ry thing

in gen'er-al (that's j.a.)

(i have thought about you

about what concerns you

—what concerns all of us
nothing's waiting for you
in the skies
                    save what yr
engineers
                    send aloft
these toys are no answer
 no answer to a man
                    swelling
in his bed   alone
cold sweat licking his balls
a man wants answers
whether a trick in bed
                    or one
in out-of-space . . .)

The dream "si formato
                    chome"
                            is what we would fly off to.
                                                    The image,
not the dream, preceded you. There is, too,
                                            the computing machine
                    another dream.
                                    All of us
have relatives we have known.
                            The moon is here
                                            and I think of it,
            save when it is
                        obscured
            by some other World's
                                intervening.
Tho' profit we do
                from these brief
                                interruptions of that light
—the lesson it teaches
                    is still there
                            —oblivious. Lost.

We have been,
                most of us,
                        badly taught
                                if history holds out to us
any evaluation of ourselves.

The World,
        which, in another resort,
                  is the last card,
      is little more than
             highly personal aberration
         —seen thru water
      or thru that other
           "a glass darkly"—
                    must, of necessity,
             take to task
                some other senses.
      'Ere we come to that other
             "Shade of a shade."
Tired Rose 'tho you are
           to adorn Her callus feet
      or Lotus to circumnavigate
           the belly.
               Beautiful

    as it is
      beautiful
        it is all of it
    some planet in celebration
          —each one
   in due proportion
        of that light.
Man,
    that acropolis you carry
        upright
          between yr legs
       will not support yr masses
              of Promise.
  You must,
      to encompass yr visions,
           steel yrselves girders.
Time & Space
    but no horizon to determine
          yr perspective now.
    There is, in the distant future,
         no point
    awaiting yr two frail lines
        —dragging
      "the fish bones out".
The crude Greeks
     crudely faced

                    the crude problems
            of their own crude world
                                    —crudely.
I, for one day even,
                cld not have endured it.
                                    Of those pre-Greeks,
                how they sufferd
                        the invaders,
                    historians leave us little.
The Indians,
            Columbus found
                    on our own continent,
                                        complete us a tale,
                    they started.
                                The Classic Tale
            along with the raving dog,
                            put to sleep. But then,
                    this is The Poem
                                & the poem,
            like a-lot-ov-other-things
                            has not yet been realized.
—With pilasters
            of ancient gimcracks
                        constructed to
            forty stories or more;
                            sonnets
                                w/ greek or latin tags
            saying nothing above a
                        Chicago financial district.
Thirty years
            forty years
                    the folly surfaces.
                                (Only in The Poem,
                    only in the middle
                            of the interrupted Poem
            do we come
                    to wing or brush stroke
                                what we know
        we have come so
                to know.

            (A CODA
            In weak times

these are strong words
but say I must,
blood swelling my pulse
or wld you prefer to have it
measured to some other?—
but then,
this is afta the event
—sober (& down)
I am ashamed
revealing
What have I reveald?
But talk
I must talk,
(sliverd tongued)
like Cassandra,
my madness upon me
I must talk
& keep on talking
'til they come and get me . . .

III

(*Time, Condition*
& *First Cause*)
I do these things that I do, for no reason
compulses me.
Tenth card. The Wheel spins in the sky. Whirls man & beast alike
thru Space, caught
in the golden cycle
—fare
& fair alike. Each one
in its own Time to define the Time
Place and Circumstance
whereby we come
to more completely identify
with these figures represented here,
ourselves,
in the Fall between the dark & the Light. The Will
—and in spite of
the grave stele that shd
point-up—after
The Expulsion from Paradise
by Masaccio

of the moving figures
                              to articulate a vernacular
                                                in the roun'
                of the landscape,
                                to reveal what's yet to be revealed.
The First card.
                The craftsman before the table
                "—Whatever he touches has some deliberate
                                & arresting character." A man
                with a mania for fixing this
                                ever-fluid whatever
                is obsessed, first, by a precise
                                definition of forms.
—"Finding our two selves
                                upon the middle of a dark way",
                                does not help. This is metaphorical device
                of a further landscape.

                                (. . . The tranquilizer is a pill
                                The disease,
                                                to be eradicated,
                must first be
                                diagnosed
                —by that blind old man & medic
                rising before the sickly death's head . . .
                —at the hock shop
                                —fixing his cup of eye:
                "Plise boys stey behind de counter"
                                whilst he examined
                my things . . .
                                "For soothsay . . .
                                                & I stepped back . . . "
At the next card,
                I do not look.
To portray the night scene,
                                mood
                                and what illumination's to be had;
                an intricate detail is introduced:

                "Watch carefully and erase, while the power
                                is still yours," . . .
Selection
                by the ear
                                man sd.

56

                    hit 'em ovah the head
                    piano player sd.
                    he aint playing right

          from the head
                              i aint playin' it no mo'
                              like 'ah use-ta
                              play it

    like the man sd.
                    that
                         & a lot-of-other things

                    ". . . wan'ta read this first part
                    now I've don'-it over (
                         no why bother showing me
                         . . . i wouldn't understan' it
                    anyway (what diff'rence does that make
                    i don't understand it myself
                                        & la betty davis here:
                    ". . . tell my fort'chune ple-ease" (or
                    the bathroom: "how do-i look?"
                    —full face ov the kabuki (but miss thing
                    tells me she aint got no kosher john
                    what's 'n nu yark goin' ta marry 'er
                                        knocking this:
          "The rush of the waves on the sea shore
                         & their recession"—how to &
        by the ear
                    like the men sd.
                              "troubles my sleep"
                    . . .)
The Drama,
          of my own creation
                              & of my own undoing
          is a complex situation. All this I know
                                        already
along with the Poem, which I know
                              to be complex too. So that
                    "What is the question"
                                        untangle it, I must
          that these conflicts in my head be
                                   resolved.
—that the hand

                              57

                    casting a shadow
            luminous
                    on the white fabrick
                        (blurr'd . . . Velasquez, might have been
                        be put to sleep.
                                    but
        (click-click-click & clack then
            knoc-knoc-knock . . . two long & one short
        cleftd tones from the stairwell
            & hail marys full ov boose
                                    charge the fosse
                    la star is here too . . . again (not the card
                    i turned down & jonnie who sd: "O Dante he
                was soft-on-us fags . . . dit-dit-dit-dah
                            —Out   all of you
                                    (still clicking) . . . yes,
                        The judgement

double -x or ex burok-rac-crasy at that . . .
            (did you know Andy Jackson couldnt even/write?
                                            yes

        but between subject and KAN-vass
                    do ya see ya stupid fag
                    I REJECTED A CARD
        & it aint kosher   it aint Vale'ethqueth
    it's painting in the lace which ya dont see   SEE
                you stupid kocksucker
    it's our own dome (the national) which aint real stone
    so gowan call the nut house let 'em come & get me
    I dont give a fuck   I have seen the true cross
                kissd the . . . Ass of Cups. The Ace of CUPS?
                    that's it   The Game is Up

Full 'ov Port—White—as not to stain my teeth
                houses the soul dont ch'ya kno. One up
        Thank you mr. Oporto for the miracle
                & to the mind-entwining Vine
                    that at times hooks
                            Her Serapht
                            . . . .

IV

To give concrete form to ideas
                                    as well as
                            a sense of move-
                                        ment to the figures,
                the moving figures in the landscape,
                                                (still Masaccio)
some disintegration must be apparent;
                                        after the separation
                the artificial separation
                                    from language.
                                                From the sensual lip
            of ambition, no word,
                            no word—only the
                                        burning fleck of light
burning in the pupil eye,
                            where he has drilled for light
                                gives an impression of
                                            alert awareness
                an awareness of eternal light
—lest we forget the eternal repetition
                    of the eye in the spread fan of the peacock
or the simplicity
                    defined on two planes
                                    with a neutral background.
                There is too
                            the rhythmic occurrence in language
                                    as the lines of the vine entwine
            in and out of the tree
                            —the lintel
                                    cross beam,
                all of which
                            terminates in the dismal heads
                                            about me.
                        (orgasm spate out
                                    & a rush of water,
                                            as it were)
In all this
                the native purity is best described
                                        into words
            lineal & dynamic. Periods?
                    we have always had them & shall
                            for a long tome to come. We

59

do not stop at them To go on
to the capitals
rising from the landscape,
to blossom at the end of lines
(old roads lead to the nearest market
classic and eclectic. The flow
of the line shd not be interrupted. The flow
of the line shd be into
coherency
—that the Scales balance & the weights be precedent.
To separate elements
by the introduction of
additional elements is to use
this opaque substance
we call reality.
The rhythmic recurrence
of accents
about the whole panorama
which is the total life of the Poem
is the total humanscape.
To trap the poem in all its
massive shapes its
stark simplicity its
brutality
—we come to Form.

here follows a Summation of Parts:

SO THAT
(SUN & MOON standing together
⊙ + ☽ ..)

As to "how do you write a poem?"
you don't
you come by stormy seas
to go to Hell in a leaky boat
losing all companions,
losing even
the shirt upon
[yr back
and with some still,
it's just a matter of
bad blood.

(but, if information be tampered with
how wld you kno?   points
—> like an arrow
to anthologists)
The flow

into coherency
not to be interrupted by
"deletions"
or just downright "dishonesty".
That the rhythmic order of Hellenes
be not imposed upon
the chaotic materials
of our daily lives,
but that we build within
a comparable state of fluidity
to meet that outer state
of fluidity;
clarity & simplicity,
the outstanding characteristics
defined upon two planes
& w/a neutral background
& that in building yr whatever
the purpose be
opaque.
Architecture (mr. Maximus)
is primarily
an art of space,
Frank Lloyd Wright;

but wld not fuse Athens or was it
Corinth w/steel. Lineal
& dynamic the line shd be
& this to be followed by
Sullivan's Law
—Form & it does not follow function.
(from here on the going's tough)
From the complex
a fundamental. The ideal is,
damn you, human.
NOTE: Jefferson replacing Athena
staying a giant
like a sonnet.

"Licht, mehr Licht", cried Goethe,
                 that is the binding medium
                     unites mortar to bricks
                         holds things together.
          (If the Poem is difficult to read
                 it's because the thought producing
                             the Poem was caboose to diesel
                                         disjunct.)
             Or would you prefer death?
                         then "turn up
          this crooked way,
                         for in that grove I lafte him."

All of which is to be followed by
                             (Orgasm V) the elongated forms
             the distortions of,
                         I supposed, later Art. Arising from
     a know-how
                 that things in themselves
                         have no meaning until
                             the imagination (events)
                                 plays w/them
         & shapes them into
                         communicative patterns.
The structural facts
             upon which rests
                     The Poem.
                         So Forth . . . .

1961

                                 V

In the Creation of the World
                     by god we have nothing to go on
except the buggin word
                 bugging us
it is only in the distance, which is time
             that we come to experience
             the act—awful as that is
             unlawful
             a break in continuity has been achieved
and we suffer from it

unable to fathom the lie,
we would
destroy the Great Work
           —releasing all stops,
      it is the keystone
of our existence
           that never sleeps

the central cortex of the arch,
             that is being
but "death is no answer"
             I agree,
for the dead come back:

                 walking among us asking
      what are these upright
                         stone slabs
           supporting a third
within the concentric circles
        What do they remind me of
that I remember
      at the summer solstice
when the dead cast their shadows
      among us

                    •

      with the central illumination we cry out
           awake in full horror
                         remembering
           of what we remember
      "that was shaped as
                 this thing is shaped"
the dead come back
           walking among us
                         asking
                         asking
      "what is the question"

                 (later, manlater)
since it has come in i let it come in

•

from whom do we conceal
                                    ourselves
                                    What?

                                                ourselves . . .)

a caged birdie poem:
                in life
            people   not   they
                    are   like   are

            in the movies
            in the movies they
            are animates
                            (dead)
                                    volition
            holds them in sway
            if ever they do meet
            in life
                    they would
                                    flip
            so imitative are we

                        •

                        an
            animated cartoon out of
                    danbury '58
                                    conn. where
            cagemates
                    "have no intellectual interests"
            except for the odds,
                    the evens are held
            checkmated by a rhyme of cells

                    blockd
                        & a confused heat
                    confused i.e., w/ a stick
        4 a.m. of a december &
                            she sits that
                            morning star upon my

                    lowest
                              window pane
                    proud
                    as might any venus
              birds meanwhile make busy like
                    their chirps of hosannas
         such consideration of the
                    oncoming light
                         and
         something too abt. Robin THAT
                    I can't read

comfort me oh these why white thoughts
                    before a green door
                              of an eastern jail where
                    even the light is automatic

und so along with the law of expediency as ref.
                    men behind bars:
                                        The Acts

                                        •

                                        mythology

                                   The Moon no. 18

              —lower than the depths

                    ? . . . . men

                              these are

                    areas of yellow and blue

                    split and forked verticals
              from sheer weight of the
                                        black horizontals

"whu'dt you get busted for"
              &
                    "be ovah ya bed t'nite baybe"
& the hunter—(this time
                    artiste (e)

   —fruithustlers
& by name miss chacha and says:
       "this moneymake runs on bread"
Chico:
    who got high on new year's nutmeg
    & begged "sheet on me babee I want to
        eet't it"
    & later released back into el barrio he
    slew his girl-wife and ripped out
      his baby's bowels

  No blame : he was
       Pure
          broken violette
      deranged
         confusion

    MISTER—franz kline 1959 oils
      big table Vol. I, no. 4, 1960
    thrusts against canvas
      but for the symbol,
         —Lost

         •

       Oblivious

         •

        sea sounds
    wave smash against the rock slime
  of the cave enclosure
      a hiss
  and chatter thrown against sand
        this:
  "Para thina poluphoisboio thalassas"

    Blockd
      , Man
    where you been this is the
     fuck'n' end
      •

> "Each one in its own Time
> to define the Time
> Place & Circumstance . . ."

old Brunswick on Boylston St. (Jack remembers) tea on the veranda
(ala Englaise) mine w/ lemon to the titter of two tiers of ladies
   who inherited their clothes if not Morgan Memorial out of the
      best attics, Back Bay Newton & Prides'. Menden Sewell & Emily
Huntington spoke of their efforts in behalf of Sacco & Vanzetti
—demonstrations before the State House & Fuller mansion on Beacon
St. Miss Menden's mother had sung at Saltzburg, a restrained Donna
Anna before she took to "bad opera" (Verdi and Puccini) for hers was
the tragic voice after the style of Muzio (Claudia) belle canto
   of second rate for she died into the Boston Opera Co. Jack
introduced Williams (Tennessee) to the Sunday evenings against
better admonitions (mine) for I was on to G.B.S. (thanks to E.P.)
   tho' Blanche is good character, social tract or not. then
too there was no excuse what w/ Eliot & Monsieur Jean in France
   as against gross misrepresentations on the New York stage.
shld say something abt virtue, rite & always subjective. "Wholly"
sd. Pound.
      wuz abt '48 or '9 ensconced on Mt. Vernon St., later
West Cedar persuing my investigations. engaged (part-time) Christian
Science Publishing House. Felix lectured on Poe at the drop of a
   hat & enticed Lancaster (John) away from "the yard" over to
      the Copley Square Boston University where to the dictates of
our hearts, we sought Her voice, arranged flowers & lived amidst
   a conglomeration of bad post victoriana w/ thanks to the
      Weinstein girls, who when we arrived at their antique shop
would close the shutters & serve their excellent ming tea while
   in defense of Poe, Felix would lecture, but for all of it we
had not got on to Melville (Olson, I think was later). so that
   even now i find the Napoleon stuffy tho' it has (twice, I think)
changed hands; frequented by store clerks (more finish than basic
stuff) turnd squires after five & god yes, the decorators. Prescott
(Townsend) abt the only remnant of this Boston still above ground,
   for as I write, the hammer falls against the best houses
      built in North America & for what? high-rise matchboxes
stood on end. Beacon Hill surrender'd to tourisme & poseur artist
on Charles St., but not for evenings spent at Don Amadon's
   excellent 18th cent. restoration on West Cedar (but still
  feel that the house fronted t'other way. possibly Revere.
a bread & cheese citizen (Don) for he subsisted exclusively

on the latter & practiced celibacy, for his was a
Calvinist morality w/ memories of hell-fire & the stocks
    about when was Corman departed for Europe & later Japan.
    . . . Annabelle supported Cid's *Origin*, first series & whose
Japanese (last time in Boston) was fluent but not his poetry
    where he cld have used it. Spicer, Blaser & Duncan not yet
on the scene, for Black Mountain was a year later. Jack
    (Wieners) shook the Jesuits that summer (circa '54). Black
Sabbaths (mine) '56 & the local constabulary calls on me:
    "having any more 'o them black masses up there, Jonas?"
    & w/ more than a few complaints about demons (incubi & succubi)
        attracted to our sessions
            . . . at that, Irish make the best mediums. a precondition:
    lore (Celtic) religion & not a little gullibility.
tho' beatnicks (later hippies were underfoot (poorly read & un-
    instructed) theirs was a total protest. round pegs don't fit
square openings—ultimately no job. still it was a Boston of land-
    marks recognizable to a Santayana. French bakery in Bay Village;
horsedrawn & the tiny Swiss bell ruckd in a spiral-like the invo-
    luted Bishop's crozier. now, like Proust, shut-in against all
this too quickly come. would I join the ladies' (of Puritanical
persuasion) resistance to removal of bricks on Beacon Hill? yes,
but to replantation of gas-lamps: a demurrer, now that junk
desperation prowls the dimly streets. & it was Joy St., (the "Barn")
    where la mama descended to us & that ole "musick-Meister" blasted
    her out of bed—all stops pull'd. Bach, may have been. Jack
(Lancaster) read the Tarots by the wrought-iron chandelier w/
        candles dipped by hand of candleman far away as Dedham. tho'
Boston could & did extend then to Pigeon Cove, where the studio
has changed hands, as has Spencer's house hemmed-in by the Boston
Music Store. few know of its location—if still. should i break
off the corners of my lines; take advantage of my rhymes? or should
    i throw in with the other side? affect a *coup de maitre*. for the
    real man (i take it) will not go yr ersatz. he will be fair.
cool of demeanor, reserved. in short; just. a few start but many
    follow along. they do not see the necessity of going into the
mind & there dig. Superficialities and mincing words over meaningless
    procedure, seldom means manhood. if you would know Nature
you'd put aside yr pots, tubes, crucible & apparatus for torturing
base metals. the all of which I wouldn't give you a that for.
    greed blinds men to truth, tho' for all of it Avery came thru;
his dignity unscathed. the Peabody blacksheep & a hazard for
    bookstall failure and always: "that Jew on Washington St"
meaning Williams or the influx of paperbacks. but i thought his

business acumen at the root of it. late as '61 or '2 still
dressed for dinner but not at the Colonial Tea Room (Charles St.)
& waitresses *cafe au lait*. his, father (after failure of the
wool market ('29) took up residence at the Harvard Club (Common-
   wealth Ave.() remarked I'd taken up with "arty people" when
I moved to the ass side of the hill. what the hell happened to
Leonard J. Feeney, S.J., Boston's Savannarolla? after they dug
that hole in the middle of the Common. & Gerrit thought my
Catullus more Martial than Marshall for then he didn't spell
it.   on the question of coons
         I shall die on the rebel side. and do not know (dark; occult)
the uses of suffering so that sooner or later find themselves
   in the enemy camp. (those predisposed to a slavery democracy
for if you scratch a bit below the surface you'll find a Jew
   or "investor" holdings whatever.

June 1968

CANTE JONDO FOR SOUL BROTHER JACK SPICER, HIS BELOVED CALIFORNIA &
ANDALUSIA OF LORCA

canto i

Spain is located somewhere between Polk Street & Laguna Beach/
   as you cross the Oakland Bridge into Portugal/
Oh, that Spicer/
     he was a flamenco, that one/
           for wld save America from
   the abuses of rime. Like Lorca (our Fedy) was 'gipsified.'
Heard 'Bird's' playing & for three years
     didn't know the taste of meat. sd. he didn't know
  music had attained to it. A tear & one blue note upon yr brow, baby.

Hated the east w/ its glib talkin' effete
     prissy espousing test-books. sd. i was John Randolph
  of American poetry, a Spanish soul brother confused by adoption
  w/ northern Europe, The American Friends & The Science & Health Book.
I thankd him ("sir") for myself & for my ancestors.

The 'amen corner' is as close as we can come to cuadro flamenco.
Walt Whitman's butterflys w/ singed wings, all silver white
     star spangled the milky-way w/ their gissem.
For then, this is Andaluz Province,
      "cadahus
        en son us"
     Tradition, you can't keep it out
  nor can you lock it under box lid.
      What is this out-cry from the dark memories,
no doubt, of the caves; animal & almost human? Cante jondo.
       Goya heard & painted it
  in all its black terror.
      Ever hear ole Manitas ('Silver fingers')
guitarrista soul?
   "Ole"
    "Vamos, Manitas!"
        "Cook, baby go!"
   poppin' their fingers (pites) & feet that won't keep still
    (baile)
      right hand for the beat like 'Jelly Roll'

   knockin' the box near the bridge (martillo)
or when he cuts loose with a bad jota & some sister from the corner

leaps to her bravura
                        & pirouettes:
                                        dat-dat-dat-dat
                    then the abrupt halt
    "Bien parado!"
                  then the fall—prostrate on the floor.
The bull fighter is the best dancer in all Spain.
The blues came into Spain with the gypsies
        who joined the jews & the moors in the Hollywood
hills back 'o El A afta the expulsion
           the which might as well be Granada!
Hey, Manitas, Jack Spicer says make with Meritas Moras,
        & the Cantaer intones the blues
             like it was early one monday mornin'
  'n i was on my way to school
          & it was the mornin' i broke my muther's rule
    "eso es cante moro"
            this cat is *bad*
 'cause the blues is bad
           from 'down home' southern Spain
where the gypsies cop their horse
       so they can wail their romances sonambules
    their canto jondo blues of sounds
            —bad sounds
    from the ballin' bad fartin' fuck sounds:
          "funky," earthy.
"gumba any you peepul from the Cape?"
          "Verde," he means.
    yeah, man, they made the step-over on the IN-flight
      to pick up on some Horace 'Silver-fingers' sides
   then hi-taild it to New Bedford
         'cause their trawler wuz waitin'
you spick like a portageese
      & the faint "th'eheres" go for broke.
Spanish? christ, i don't even speak English!
       "ahh yeah, i got my mo-joe workin' for you."
   "'cause ah bin to the gypsie   git my fort'chun tole"
    "she say some other man come in de back way"
    "when ah leaves for wurk by de front"
Spicer, we want a big round sound in poetry
         like Ammons gets from a horn,
    or Picasso's high voltage line
        execution of a picador.
But gone. over & done with. forget it.

Jack Spicer fled Boston as Lorca fled Nueva York.
     so 'un-latin'
          'no magic'
       saved only by Walt Whitman
              "tu barba, llena de mariposas"
     & sleeping with his back to the Hudson.
The cantaer's voice couldn't pierce the horror of norte americano silence
     broken only by the jing-jing of the cash register.
       so Saeta
          no cante moro
            no blues
              nuthin'
You know, us latins come to take on frightnin' implications
     confronting northern insensibility.
I adopt your style, personality-deliberately a mask. " . . . the
                (only escape from
    the hatfaced bargainer & money-changers."

        canto ii

Jack Spicer says wait, don't leave, the poem's not over yet.
They also say that Europe stops abruptly at the Pyrenees.
Spicer says they mean the California-Nevada line.
Yellow wind
       i've seen you mount the green night
           thru the spines of moon fleckd trees
    in the half-light.
       "duende"
         "duende"
           & yells of: "Man,
              he's got it"
        & another: "he's got it"
From then this is Andaluz province. Spicer sd: "doan yew talk to me about j-azz."
Flamenco came up the Mississippi afta it
       buried its black roots under a N'Orleans cat house.
  "hey, momma gimme a taste 'o that fine ty'ass you're swingin'"
    "yass yass yass" 'n that's tjazz
      that's duende
          for they talk of nothing else
     save "duende"
        "duende"
   who's got it
      who aint—be it Manitas

de Plata's guitarrista

                or Picasso's advertisements of the tribes

   & folly, as thousands roar:

                "Man, he's got it"

                          "he's got it"

        "i tell you that cat cooks"

                "tellin' you like it is"

     "got flamenco"

           ("that's a little shit in yr blood")

    Fedy (Garcia Lorca)

            a lame, like all poets, a memory of a roar

from the mouth of the Hudson & Harlem rivers

                      later, spat out in Havana harbor

more than likely, the bad afta taste of it all

        but rememberd Harlem

           where he heard some cante moro, faintly

All over America the little magazines conspired

    to board Jack Spicer up in a California Street rooming house,

  for lack of space.

          "duende"

           "duende"

                —elbow nudged ribs & a wink:

        "yeah, he's got it"

      "aw man, he's black with it"

                  & "wont quit it"

       "kno what you mean"

Miles heard it (Sketches of Spain) like Casals like

             de Falla, "you kno"

        "jes goes without saying"

      Santayana understood it "but, (hunch of shoulders)

         he's escolastico, si?" (another province, anyway)

And so it goes. Life, Death, Love, el Toro &

              "duende"

                 "duende"

        all they discuss

          ones who have it

          ones who do not

"yes, yes, yes, Senor, eso es"

When Garcia Lorca came to New York the Stock Market held firm

    & the trains ran on time as usual. The jews along 125th street
sold condoms full of gentile dreams to the black crocodiles in their
stores.

"this cat's so bad
he'd cut his own muther
if she got on the stand."
that's black singing. "eso es canto moro"
negros, negros, negros, negros
envoi
Here's to a green river
doing a belly-crawl thru
yr blood thirsty sod,
Andalusia
& red bells undulating the crests of yr yellow wind
weaving thru the green blades
of fixd bayonets (poor Spain)
bristling in yr geld'd landscape/by
overhead the plowd furrowd brows
of darker gods hover:
Toledo in a Storm
Sleepy Fedy among the olive groves
where I imagined they planted you
"adiosito"
a whisper of yellow wind   rattles the dry
teeth
in the skull of a dead horse's mouth
—a shudder of leaves
"adiosito"
red bells thru the soft wind:
"adiosito"
"good-nite"

GLOUCESTER
(Impressions for J. W., III)

As to a trumpet blast
      reawakened I return to
places once visited. Old names, streets
and familiar sights revive of the instant.

Thus are we judged by
                former knowledge, arising now
fresh bloomd,
      from beneath the past tense of
the subjective cemetery.

Riding, riding, still riding back
              the subjective omnibus.

Returning from Manchester when
Mrs. Butler was alive (God rest her)
with Richard (my ole da et cetera) to
Oak St., Gloucester. A fine old house
as his grandfather left it:

          Clapboard, Queen Anne, Federalist
door brass as the eagle spread; colonial
ladder-backs; the floor eight or more
inches wide, the boards were. Several
generations on the lapd and with horror of
                  horrors
conceald in every closet.

        His mother a fit of starts and stops
and was shockd that I wanted to go over
to East Gloucester's
              Jazz at Storyville moved to
North Shore of the summer. But my "dicky"
suggested instead we go up to see how
        Our Lady was doing.

            ("Our Lady" (to cue you) was signal to
            get the old man's car keys and hi tail it
            over to Rockport where the ritual of

                                        the highly mystical quarry
              of los abandonadas.

                                        And on weekends
              nearly half of
                        Harvard's Divinity School.   )

And it is said that
                        Rockport's a dry town.
There were other moments too as
                        when the Blessing of the Fleet and
She goes down to the sea.
                        Rose & anemone petals
trail out to sunset   red
                        in the afta glow.

                                        There was
the studio in Pigeon Cove where Eleanor
                        (divine name) declaimed me
"The Four Quartets."

                        I was brought to my knees
and so it was that I decided for Poetry.

Also there was the matter of
                        the Old Saltzberger (Old salt in
Gloucester Harbor) and the Burgomaster
we need not go into.
                                        But the cruise about
the harbor of a Sunday and the summer houses
                        nestled in the cliffs of Annisquam
stay with me.

There was more, much more, tho' mostly
              s'amuse a s'amuse.   Memory she is also
mother of the Muse.
                        So that The Judgment
that might be finality,
                        is no more than
Her flowers reawakened   to delect us.
                                        My friend,
shall we partake further
                        of that mortal odor?

76

COMPLAINTE DE L'OUBLI DES MORTS

> . . . man the dead
> 's in the boneyard
> they don't get around
> much anymore.
> J. Laforgue

In a loft facing a parking lot
   on a main drag of the tired
southend, lives my friend
   the fellow artist stumbling thru
dope-filled mornings he's
             not ready for:
dried-up paint pots, brushes
      stiff'ning has managed
(Mercury 'by nite') to avoid the eight to five
he produces us no picture.

Outside ghosts ply the streets
      ring door bells where no one's home
winos with eyes for nickles & dimes
   children like vomit rail
      at the street corners the sharps
& flats of their vagrancy
crumpled bags brown &
          white emerge from the rooming
houses & disappear
around corners that indicate
nothing.

1965

THE STREET

it's a nice street
                    I live on a very nice street
w/nice little ole ladies
                    who remark on yr
window boxes
                    & go on to say what a nice day
it is for death

they have dividends
                    & memories of horse cars
                              on Tremont St.;
Cora Fletcher who de-
                    scended from the Revolution
rest assured
                    Heaven is of the reformed
                                        persuasion
with English place-names
                    skirting the periphery

1966

BROTHERHOOD & ALL THAT BAD AIR

Theology the which
    has never been my bent
       is non-theless
not odious to me

      for I feel an
affinity w/these
        non-essential un-
exploited   who congregate
at this inter-
      section
  in the south-end of the city
they are my own flesh & blood
        everything
they pass is Communion
       whether it be
the tobacco sac
      or a pint of cheap
   muscatel they drink

      below their backs
the road beds
   of the N.Y., N.H., & Hartford Ry.
    inviting you to emigrate
—out to California say
     to San Francisco now

where the writers
   & related sister Arts
           assemble

pretending a Parnassus

MORPHOGENESIS
(being a conventionalization of
"Morphemes" of Jack Spicer)

clearly outlined
men & things stand out
in a realm where
                    everything is visible
no contour is blurrd.
here is a device of essential
                    explanation:
        retarding the foot
        the going back & forth
it is the quiet existence
of things according to
                    their natures.
nor are we robbd of our
        poetic natures
the effect is
precisely that
they describe
what is brought to light
in perfect fullness
in that
a continuous
   rhythmic procession
            of phenomena
                        passes by
in cinematic exhibition
fragmentary or half-
            illuminated, we glimpse
the pathos of
heretofore unplumbed depths
the which once long ago
        a boor enlarged into
        parenthesis,
        voluminous &
                    syntactical.
So that God, its three selves,
give in and quietly
        disentangles Himself
from a syntactical
        subordination to the Word,
no longer made flesh.

(abt here i am fully aware
            that this is not the world of awakeness)
The old woman now touches
    it, equally free
            the new present which
continues unchallenged
until, with verse
            (The Law) once again
to break the scene off.
All content is arranged with
that end in view.
"I" is the recollection
which awaken in future
                dream tenses.

So that the possibility of
    connections before and after
no longer exist(s). It is
an old story made
        the exclusive present.
So it was
after these things
he said:
    "Behold, here I am".
Seaweed & seascum
    bedringgled (bedraggled) the
        wholly transformd.
It is the voice of the line
coming from that dark place
to foreshadow in
    a foreground
our eyes are not yet
            accustomed to;
these sentences about whose
syntactical connections
    we are told nothing.
It is the mysterious(ly) wary.
Therein lies its motivation.
The entire process
    in vacuo
no place is meant to indicate
        clearly.
The time is always
        late in the evening

it's "the early morning"
that is the wordless spectre
    we wrestle a skin-diver
in a room full of blood.
The place we shall
come to know
is clearly stated
    in certain musical
    statements of
        horns upendings.
(I take it that Jack Spicer's "phonemes" carry
        the printed circuitry that upon utterance
        reproduces the visual impression)
The place of the Act is
exactly stated.
It is a scene characterized
  apart from person
or story.
neither pleasant or unpleasant
is all we are told
  & is seldom if ever
illuminated in old script.
Crabbd ambiguity of
  lost connections.
The contrary indicates the
  absolute existence.
Suspense is the present
  bordering on the future.

The Poet robs us of
    our emotions;
we are left fishbones
    wrangling by seaboard.
This is the "two" used of
      direct discourse.
Thought indication bares
      its motives.
We are still but not free
      Of guilt.
When the fever passes
  we contrive to give up
    the host.
God is an interruption of
    heavy silence.

The two "went together".
Everything, you see, remains
            unstressed.
The "two" equally ancient
     in the foreground.
The brush-strokes pock marks,
     the lacuna of Rodin.
What lies between light
    spaces undefined?
This detail of canvas is
   undisclosed silence
        going back & forth
           leaves an impression
So instantly we reawaken
This is the first day of our lives!

BACK 'O TOWN BLUES

There is a bourgeois dullness
             that settles plumb blank upon
the blobs of american cities

it is a dullness of locality
& to each city its own brand
             of *ennui*

i have felt it
   so must have you
the traffic of a thorough-fare
      moves left to right
                     & right to left
         thusly the faces in windows

                  move likewise
or they loiter abt stoops
         or congregate
at the corner's intersections

(anticipating violence) what else
save read a book on the Index
            or see a controversial movie
dead tho' they move

                  like an Egyptian mummy
whose guts have been excerpted
i tell you

            there is a bourgeois
dullness
that settles plumb blank upon
the blobs of american cities

1965

DILEMMA II

if you come right down to it the
              hemmed-in Proteus the
                    lopsided whale
                              stranded on a California
                                    beachhead, people
milling about all
                    phenomena—
critical poem
                    saying the
                        upside-down cake
                    not in the sky that
                        canvas of surprise
              no, hidden within sub-
                              terranean
                    remoteness of human
                                    ingenuity
To save? again no
                    to venerate the
dastardly;
              (that's innovation
without right.) the
      minute is found within
the narrow confines of space
where the ever lurking
              presence of Time: the
myriad colors with
grounded principles like
              as Michael Angelo down
                              on all fours mixing
                              the Sistine ceiling with
                    universal dirt. unity? you say
yes, but where will you
              find unity unless you
sacrifice space
that diction of rhetoricians
                    like a backslider with
double barrel'd nerve.
              we lend encouragement after
              the fact.
                    known? who

85

knows the Eternal outlaw
can safely say he
knows nothing.

1959

FOR JOHN WIENERS 1/6/60

who will come after you
        singing as well/
                here the music breaks

                                as you

        (later we must take that
                again make it reprieve)

                                sound

        like a black iris by Kline
                a broken telephone
        (old kind with horizontals
                and forkd receiver

                                for hooks

        to receive the (click) poem
                it rings but it is
                not for the(e)
        (head full of old tunes
                w/a bad connection)

                                fix? why
                                hell noe

        suffer there for me to

                                suffer.
                                whats?

        if this music hits you hit
                                back

        we go straight too
                but hell
        that is too
w/me it is the same old wrong number

                                up . . . . .

man sd. (Groliers') we got
audience one old *measure*
some last yrs' ferlinghetti
& a corman revue achilles fang
rummaging thru I heard from
corman & remembered ch'you then
the old cat connectd & laid it
on me man I flippd the upshot wuz
yr ole lady on the phone
blaming dana

87

when, man, it's the beads O
stop up the drain
and the access to remorse
too
there is no loss of
whiteness in yr hostelerie
be it wentley or irvington
rooms they all have
spaces   between
the fuckin' wall paper rhymes

1960

WORD ON MEASURE

In the beginning: The Word
                    imperfect—half meaning half longing
                but for the Poem of the Fairy
                            like wings to fly off on
            If we Measure
                        we reckon on fairydust
            what rubs off the word
                                Measure that
            the rest
                    Silences
Being: (my little light knows me)
                            IS—Life
                        a verb and w/o Measure &/?
IF the poem
            'if' anything—becoming—not become
                            that sounds under glass
        IS-ing
                hums like a bee
The Poem's a very
                light Measure
                        'er rer
                            A Dance—yes!
                    thank you Dr Williams
            that's spontaneous
                            Celebration
            the noisy 'brat' with brassy b's
                                makes it
            Shit the intellectual sun
                is nothing but

                            a complete collected warehouse
            it's the consumer Poem
                            what takes and makes it
                which is something else
                                SEE-IN?

Expanding 'word on measure' to include sometime that's 'prose' but not
always—which is the dream be it super or economy minded and or where
as I could go on in the head and make this thing's head a poem but I had it
down before a sort of long hand job you see I type them after I do them the
first time

How measure word

          that's IF within measure

                     without we have

         already the earth's circumference

         many times over

The Poem within without measure

      NO, matter is what we reckon by time

    that we some set our watches to

                  'TIME'

        and we some strain to see the thing

which has recently become Space all because

        the high rate of travel—to me is holding

to a certain sticking place

           like Chung's middle rotating

      within   about a certain point

Thus Distance is reflecting

This way   we never actually make it

                'So good' the I suppose maker

           says: 'you won't fly off—nowheres'

. . . Which who was it Bergson says we can't imagine 'nothing'

but he Bergson was no Poet he had to make it without

So I don't follow him either

You see Jack I'm like those cats on the Wheel of Fortune

  I won't let go—(hey, those cats aren't real people)!

    —it's more over to what I said to Jack-the-measurer

  about kikes being half human half rat and not all black

But then most of us are fairies except C . . . . . whose origin

is history and says in no. 15 he's glad as happy not being one

then went on to get himself mixed up in Miss Moore's Fables

  which I didnt like because we have our own things going

here uncle Remus and little black sambo you know push the

home products like the thin man who's on junk like all

  almost 100 per cent americans who aren't really there as gone

  are

        So Fairies to get back to us don't laugh Mr. W.B.

  Yeats could see them in fack dug them in his garden

Spicer says 'Butterflys' but he's mad as a Californian

and that's not because it's nowhere which is really not is

So who wants to imagine that

              better measure

               the word as you might a fairy

          if you saw one like: so big or

                    so tall

was it a good fairy or a bad one—but that's how much can

you put up with some people think all fairies bad but
that's northern which I have a speck of—

                        the rest of me southern
   the Irishers are the worse they have them green and say they
stash away gold this sounds jewish to me and we have a
    few of those kind too like lennie who is always flying off to
    New York or Provincetown but then he's not a real fairy
I hear he's a fag who beats up guys anyway he goes to a
    psychologist which is hoax for Rabbi or Priest not alf
our american fairies are so mixed up mostly they are white tho
there are a few colored ones but they can't be trusted much
  like the taffy colored frog that took five dollars from
  marshall's wallet who really wanted to convert him into a
white church—not catholic that's painted black by that english
Queen (a real one) well I don't need to tell you history
  no it was not marshall he took it from Rex who is a big
queen—dont confuse with the tudor bitch who was not a big
  queen like Rex but a Real one

                back to the Poem
                      I push
                              the beginning is all

                  uphill
                       so compulsed am I to light
         I am becoming a
                  bigger bean sprout
                            each day
      The poet is a surprise to
                 every one
        including me
                Life is full of everything
   eye can lay hold of
             to me Free like Time
      I get by sending back a
                  self addressed envelope
        saying I'll pay later
                    but I won't mr luce who has
      everything under control
               well he can just keep his Fortune
      which really is nothing
                but a big wheel's report
                anyhow

THE MUSIC MASTER (*after a Mozart divertimento*)

Tho' I cannot offer you
my not *too* unsumptuous bed, bring
on to me yr verses.   We must
find yr metric.   Your dark eyes
do not fool me. Tell me more abt
your "false start". Don't
chop yr things into
                    separate iambs. Use
the music of
the streets.   Did he,
I mean, seduce you or you
he, (is that correct? I mean
            grammar-wise. Corman wld be
                    horrified.)
Naturally, yr rhythmic structure
what the hell could that tell you
            that we don't
                        already kno.
You shd have been my
        Swinburnian 'miss'. This
will land us both, Guido,
        tho', "Tony", pardon me,
            in Dante's sodom's mist.
And "dont" & I quote E.P.,
        " . . . imagine that a thing
will 'go' in verse because
it's just too dull to 'go' in prose".
Would, that I cld
        entwine abt you naked
                alexandrines. That's
a little light song.   "Don't
get the wrong
"Dawn in russet mantle
                clad". That's bad.
Too viewy. Letz be frank (not O' blank blank
                wonder what
                    his approach'd be? 'baby, like
I've got eyes'. Don't
at the end of lines make

    ev'ry line stop dead then
with a heaving sailor's hump

                    begin the next. We must
become
          musicians of
                    the imagination.
                    Alliteration,
                              you must
hear yr language spoken.
Drest, & be discreet
(upon the street) but in the pad,
               en dishabille
                    let the bedsprings creake.
Marvel. Question. or some
          other creep. Let the
neophyte kno
                    assonance. (the watch
          or was it the clock.) He must "go"
"that's it
          for today, baby."
Now he calls me "baby".
This to be follow'd by
          my dishy
     sister's voice:
          "did-DENT you
               make him
                         YET?" Hell noe
besides, he's straight. Letz go
ovah to grease alley
          and may his whores,

                         in the mornings,
snore at him.   (&
               "publish this"? Who cares? anyway
          my folks can't read.

93

A THEME

September
"and the scattered leaves of all
                    the universe" lie—in
unused crumples across the grass
and benches green as once were they
now the cessation of all
                    creative activity
startled from time to time by a wind
that is moved by its passion
a scene at once too studied and poetic
to be long endured
        as it were some conversation
that is flowing
        endlessly downhill
the thoughts veer as the wind does

1960

FRAGMENTUM, 1957

. . . did you ever hear
             the bronze Apollo
cullen sing?

             mighty lak a rose
tho' not in that dey. Christ!
             those 'skeeters
at Walden Pond

             but they kept yellin':
"Steve, it's row-mantick"
             but Wieners
said nothin' that year   for wrote
      in his journal
                   while i went
quite frankly out of my wits
assailin' jews w/ ovens

& the coons w/ White citizen's
             retaliations. well,
it's still a free society,

             ain't it?

1967

FOLLOWING THE SAME ROUTE BUT AT A DIFFERENT PACE

. . . in some ways you do
       frankly astound me
now you take timmy
     that's the next door cat:
four puffs of white feet
       pads up and down
thru the dead leaves
    stop a little here a
       little there to poke his
nose under then a pounce
     to send the pigeons by
onto a great scurry of wing flaps
    that take to the naked
        branches above;
what could he find
    there to interest him so?
    I remember the area
      from last summer
—bare as a bone's ass
    save for spots of grass
     & tree roots humps
from beneath

    —back to the Greeks
who like the freudians
   had a word for
      everything
& Gertrude Stein noted: we do like
   to call names. no
   I want to be free
    uncategorized the—
X factor   the elusive neutron
    not to be tagd and
shut between musty volumes
   on shelves above
heads of bookworms
    read but not quite "QUICK"
"the door"   (door halfclosed
   he makes it
    the train (his) is waiting
   I continue as I was.

1964

4 POEMS OF MYSELF & OTHERS

i

In every Circle there is
        some romantic design:
An old man half-blind de-
        claiming his fragments
of Sappho
        to streets too assiduous
in their stupefaction to believe
        Greek flung in the face of
public speech,
        that's just plain old
American
        defying scansion
Lacking malice,
        there is no presumption
here. The emotions
        have not been challenged
the pride
        still intact
due to a language
        barrier. A
demonstration of force has been
        avoided. The hound
sensing nothing
        above curb-stone level
trots merrily on
        wagging a tail of
contentment

ii

Search for a just
        terminology but
the blood has
        long ceased to flow
in the sentence.
        Saint
and genius does not appear:
        there are interruptions
between the Acts

and the long gaps of
silences. Tho
        I lack the saint's vision, I have
the Poet's damaged ear.
        O World
of the False Vision
        O all you
eastman kodax people
        —film under water scene.
Of the seven loaves
        to the multitude he
subjectively said:
        "let them be fed", something
which they have not
        themselves created. 'Bon appetite'
and their imaginations
        grew.
A child
        I remember
opening shell after shell of god
        who eats the things
—clams, finding no pearls.
        About now I had
other failures: I heard
        the sirens singing
from the spiral shell.
        And I remember yes
my first image burst
        into bloom.
Other moments there were too
        come back to me now
as I write: there's my
        first love in a dress of
gold brocade and there
        the Rose
its double meaning of
        convoluted intent,
set me all contra-basso
        vibrating about the one
string the which was
        all my counterpoint.
Something of their meaning
        has been lost. It is
an age of Comedy.

iii

Memory
          mother of the Muses:
"I remember, I remember", that
          was my father
"and when you are older"
          holding on/to words
for fear of losing his mind,
          —meaning words
"you'll be
          sorry *one* day"
But I was on
          a roller coaster and
the rides on the house. The question mark
          was too far out for me
nor did those jewels
          arrayed along the shelves
keep me from my rage. I
          remember too, how my first
Poem brought me to
          my knees.

iv

Today
          most men come at bargain rates.
It is
          not their faults, but
circumstances
          making for a shift in
          emphasis. Men today are
sleek
          and rich in flesh-tones.
It is all reflection
          from shallow pools
and it is already late
          September. Approaching
the Dark Lady between the Twin Towers,
          B & J, they stammer,
long lapses of silence or
          they panic. They do not have
the Magic Word or
          they have lost it.

A REVEL
(for John Fusco)

delirious as tho
of barbitos
                    i had drunk
& a strange passion
                            swelling blood into my heart
from my mind
                    runs the Poem
upon dithyrambic feet
                    lustily
i cry out in a Poem to you

                            my sweet will be twenty
                            on sunday next
upon such feet
                    of shaggy measure
i come
        privily
                permitting
                        it pleases you
a scene by Fragonard
prostrate
            to whisper to you
beneath a hedge
as above & about hover
nymphs, niads & other
                        demi-beasts of sorts
even to the hushd wings
                    of pretty doves
            fluttering & cherubs
caroling
        my amours
                repeat
                        my sweet will be twenty
                        on sunday next
now in middle March
        when the wind
                    is intemperate still
  i muster what devices
the imagination prompts me to
(a painter, these conceits are
    not unfamiliar to you)

so i need not
                    make apologies for
a decor
            classic & eclectic
which, in my frenzy
                        i arranged
        hoping therewith
to ensnare your fancy, sweet
it is a Poet's madness
                        driving him
willy nilly
howbeit to his own destruction
                maskd or
                        metamorphosed into
some wondrous animal guise
centaur, unicorn or faun
                repeat
                        my sweet will be twenty
                        on sunday next
so even to the birds
                    whose calls
the ancients invoked
            & unabashedly coo'd
            their canzones
                        to wit-a-woo
all of it i bring
            again, my sweet, to you
in the spring-time of the Poem
where else
                when spray begins to springeth
could i come in my folly
                bearing you
in some small measure
such snatches
                purloind as i have
of that antique liturgy
                    repeat
                        my sweet will be twenty
                        on sunday next
the phrase as reprieve
reverberates within my skull
as i say in my high passion
        may he not also
                    love me too

repeat

my sweet will be twenty
on sunday next

& i have come to sing to you

1961

A WIDOW'S LAMENT (afta the Chinese)

in the eighth luna month
    you, mi lord departed
out thru the west gate.
        the lazy flys
have come and gone
          since last I had word
  of you.
          (heavy), i sit beneath the
rotten pear tree.
The Third Immortal Maiden foresaw
        your return;
               hence,
i shall do my thread-work here
    looking ever to the east
            lattice.

1961

. . . is what I keep asking myself

that night mr. Roosevelt got reelected as far back as I can remember mr. Roosevelt was getting himself reelected mother and aunt Loretta who signed her letters Anna Loretta Rios-Olive because she said the Rios-Olive is as important to America as the Perkins and Parkers she meant miss Rosa Parker whose mother was a Perkins and miss Parker had books with marked pages to show what the Perkins and Parkers did to help mr. Washington free us from the English kings as later the Parkers gave all their money to help Maud's folks get free from the Southerners but aunt Loretta said this was not so and they aunt Loretta and miss Parker with all of her books and the marked pages would say things about the English kings and the Southerners until mother's head would suggest itself and they would apologize and miss Parker would leave and aunt Loretta would read mrs. Eddy for mother so her head wouldnt suggest itself anymore and uncle Ed would come home as he did this night and tell us mr. Roosevelt is mr. it for another four years mother and aunt Loretta didnt like mr. Roosevelt but Maud did and when I went to Maud's room which was before hers mine she was humming and the radio was talking about how mr. Roosevelt did it mother and aunt Loretta liked mr. Roosevelt's cousins whose uncle was elected before this mr. Roosevelt now always getting himself reelected but aunt Leona from St. Augustine who later came to live with us didnt like the other mr. Roosevelt before this mr. Roosevelt now always getting himself reelected since I can remember for what he did in San Juan to the fine families like her husband's and all the trash came in and they had to live in St. Augustine with grandfather and granny Lizzy who was so old nobody knew how old she was and used to talk with all our dead relatives for us because she was the only one that could see them well not really see them because she was blind and she said I had blond hair and fair skin which I didnt but I was told not to say I didnt so I didnt and uncle Ed said she was soft as a grape but uncle Ed was father's brother and aunt Loretta said they were mixed up with the worst protestant element in New Bedford so the men had salt on the brain aunt Loretta was right because uncle Ed thought a lot about the sea and always said he was a fisherman when people asked him what he did but there was no water in Plainfield and they could not understand uncle Ed saying he was a fisherman all the time and uncle Ed would change the subject and talk about something else and nobody would say anything because we all knew a lot of things that we didnt talk about and everybody knew that should know so nobody would say anything when uncle Ed started being a fisherman all over again like the summer he took me out to Nantucket to mr. Enos who went to school with father in New Bedford and they drank beer and talked about the old days and the mess mr. Roosevelt was making and they asked me how I liked Nantucket and I said I didnt and they said that my grandfather would turn over in his grave and I guess they were right cause father said grandfather was hit over the head and drowned near somebody's lighthouse off Gloucester so later uncle Ed gave me a copy of Moby Dick and then I knew why uncle Ed was always a fisherman and didnt go to the Health Society with mother and aunt Loretta and said the Monitor had no guts and aunt Loretta would read because she said uncle Ed was highly suggestive like Maud who got flu and mrs. Glickman's doctor came to our house to make her better and talked mother into examining her and told uncle Ed mother had tumor aunt Loretta was in New York raising money for the real Indians who lost their rice crop and when she got back she told Maud that mrs. Glickman's doctor should not have come to our house and the practitioner came over from Greenwich and then mother got happy again and then people started suggesting death to us first aunt Leona in New Bedford where she was cremated and then great uncle Fred but great uncle Fred was Catholic like some of father's people and they cant get themselves cremated like father who was not a practicing Catholic then mr. Roosevelt no first mr. Roosevelt got himself reelected and then he died and they played good music on the radio and when the train passed thru 30th St. station I cried with George Dayhof who cried driving back to York from Philadelphia and all the good music was playing on his car radio but we couldnt hear it at his house in York as his people are Quakers and dont like radios but they liked me and I went to their church which they call a meeting house and nobody said anything except one man who got up after a while and talked from the audience and nobody was surprised as they are not at aunt Loretta's Health Society when she got up one Wednesday evening and told everybody how Science saved our house from mortgage and we didnt ever have to go to mr. Roosevelt's house loanman in the First National Bank Building because aunt Loretta didnt think well of mr. Roosevelt who died after father suggested death to us and didnt because the Practitioner came from Greenwich and everything was as it should have been and the Practitioner left us to our goodness but Maud was humming as she hummed the whole time the Practitioner was with us to get things back where they should be after so many people suggested death to us and didnt and uncle Ed didnt accept father's suggestion because he talked with mr. Degrutta the Practitioner and he later went with aunt Loretta to the Health Society that was then the First Church of Christ, Scientist because they had enuf members to become aunt Loretta told Maud not to be telling people like mr. Carney that father died and we cremated him at night in Westchester as she did and she was not to discuss our home life with mrs. Glickman who was an outsider but Maud was sorry as she said she was but aunt Loretta said she was colored and colored people had colored love so they had a good deal to overcome but that's not what uncle Ed said uncle Ed said Maud had bad nigger blood and wasnt like mrs. Homan who went to the Health Society and her husband was a dentist in the colored section of the Army but when Captain Homan came home from the Army he wasn't colored at all he had blue eyes and fair skin like aunt Lizzy said I had and I didnt because I went back in father's people and everybody talked a good deal about the Homans but after a while they stopped and started talking about the Germans and then miss Olga came to us and everybody started talking about miss Olga and said she was German but miss Olga was not German miss Olga was Swiss and the Swiss dont like the Germans very much because miss Olga told us how they used to dump bread over the border when the Germans insulted them because they wouldnt exchange their old marks aunt Loretta liked miss Olga's coming to us because she could talk French and German and aunt Loretta liked talking in French and German because aunt Loretta was a governess where they talk French and German so they talked German better but I didnt understand German because aunt Lizzy said German was the pig's language but uncle Ed said aunt Lizzy was soft as a grape so that was that Maud said mrs. Glickman was German too but miss Olga spoke with mrs. Glickman and said she was a Pole and her people Jews but I didnt understand that and she didnt look like a Pole to me but Maud liked mrs. Glickman and was always saying how much more money she made when she worked for mrs. Glickman but aunt Loretta said mrs. Glickman liked Maud but she wouldnt have her working for her because she talked too much and couldnt afford to have Maud around talking so much but mrs. Glickman was a great talker I dont know why aunt Loretta said Maud talked too much Maud didnt talk too much Maud hummed Maud was always humming when everybody else was talking too much but mrs. Glickman didnt hum mrs. Glickman talked everytime I'd see mrs. Glickman on the street she was talking so much Maud came to us from mrs. Glickman and mother and aunt Loretta was not sure Maud was right for us coming from mrs. Glickman and miss Kirkland from the Health Society told mother and aunt Loretta that Maud would bring bad vibrations in our house and it was bad enuf having uncle Ed's vibrations that werent bad but werent as vibrations should be and everybody was trying to fix uncle Ed's vibrations but uncle Ed didnt care a hoot about damn fool women and their ole vibrations and he told mr. Schofield at the post office he didnt mother said Maud wasnt anything before she came to Plainfield not even a Baptist but aunt Loretta said this could be good but miss Kirkland wasnt so sure and so Maud came to us from mrs. Glickman who wasnt a Quaker before she was a Christian Scientist mrs. Glickman wasnt ever any of these things for uncle Ed said she wasnt anything like Maud and that was very well because Maud wasnt anything but miss Olga said mrs. Glickman was a Pole and she miss Olga talks a little but I didnt understand mrs. Glickman being a Pole do that I didn't understand Maud humming like that and not saying anything uncle Ed said Maud didnt understand either and aunt Loretta said Maud hummed because all colored folks hummed to fill up their head since their wasnt much else in their heads so thats why they gave us all the wonderful spirituals that aunt Leona could play in St. Augustine on the gold piano that great uncle Vaz brought from San Juan with his wife and children when the other mr. Roosevelt before this mr.

Roosevelt now always getting himself reelected since I can remember let all the trash come in and ruin everything so the fine families had to come to Charleston and New Orleans where cousin Edmund comes to us from once removed aunt Loretta said cousin Edmund was once removed because he was great uncle Vaz's people and great uncle Vaz's people had renegade blood and was always causing revolutions and I guess she was right because cousin Edmund caused everybody in Plainfield to talk and miss Kirkland said cousin Edmund had a cavalier dash and I didnt understand anything about cavaliers but I liked cousin Edmund because I wanted to be tall like he was and have sideburns and black hair but mother said I couldnt ever because I had brown hair and we werent supposed to be very tall so that was that but I still wanted to but I didnt say anymore about it but cousin Edmund promised to send me boots and ten gallon hat like he always wore in New Orleans but he didnt never because he aunt Loretta said couldnt go over to New Orleans because he had trouble with mr. Long so cousin Edmund had to go to Cuba where uncle Ed said his wop friends were hiding out from mr. Long and I didnt understand anything about all these things but I didn't understand a lot of things about cousin Edmund being at our house as aunt Loretta said people in Plainfield wouldnt understand because of Maud but I didnt understand that either because cousin Edmund liked Maud and said she belonged in New Orleans and Maud giggled which wasnt like Maud who always hummed and Maud didnt hum when cousin Edmund came to us once removed since cousin Edmund's coming Maud giggled so aunt Loretta and mother talked with uncle Ed and then aunt Loretta read while uncle Ed talked to cousin Edmund in the back parlor where nobody could hear them and I was reading what I dont remember what I was reading and mother was trying a new pattern she got from miss Olga and aunt Loretta was as I said she was reading and uncle Ed was in the back parlor standing in father's shoes as mother said he was suppose to well not really father's shoes because mother gave father's things to the Salvation people who dont kill like the army that father and uncle Ed was and went off to help the fine families make mr. Zapata behave so father gave uncle Ed his gold watch to look out for the women and me so when uncle Ed keeps taking out his watch and looking at the gold chain we knew uncle Ed was turning over something that would be as father would have it so nobody said anything this night until uncle Ed raised his voice in the back parlor and opened the french doors and then he and cousin Edmund had a glass of Sherry which father kept and called Jerry because its Spanish and then uncle Ed would clear his throat and address mother and aunt Loretta as ladies and say as he did this nite that cousin Edmund has to leave us very suddenly this very night and mother and aunt Loretta would make a fuss and say he must come again and cousin Edmund said he would but we knew he wouldnt as he was going to Cuba where there was sure to be trouble as there was and mr. Ricardo's father lost out and mr. Ricardo has to teach ladies Spanish and French at the Berlitz System in New York so he couldnt finish his book on voodoo that he was always writing but aunt Loretta was certain it all worked out for the best as she felt it was all mesmerism and we should see it for what it is but I didnt understand very well about mesmerism and mother said it was just as well as aunt Loretta had seen it all through along with mrs. Eddy for us so we wouldnt have to bother read mr. Ricardo's book that was never finished anyway but uncle Ed wasnt so sure since he was down in Mexico where the Indians go along with all this mesmerism that aunt Loretta could see through with mrs. Eddy and they were Christians at the same time

TO A STRAYED CAT

5 months you were destitute
Destitute
          and w/o that traffic of loves
who now pursue U
I took you in
yr verses I taught
             my acute footwork
yr sentences to perculate
the flute and woodnotes wild
           to pipe and trill
instructed you the skill
               of the metric
                  well turn'd
               the unalterable line
to refine
Ah, but that was, as you'd say,
"the past" and anyhow now
                in the 'big city' you have
attracted numerous critics of whome
one has recently
            anthologized you
"doom of Atreus"
But the bed you slept in
            does not lie vacant
new fauns have come to my crags
            to try my tender fern shoots
Let there be deep woods between us
and a briar thicket impasse
              in the beyond.

SONG AFTER WALLER, HERRICK & OTHERS

Go
    tell her that waits
or him that bides
his time to cease
        that coral lips to fade
and amber studs
         shall lose their hold
            that bind
you from that sacred
                tryst
many the rotted bowl
       that went unbowed
many the virginal
             to rust
       unplucked
but eye shall burn
       what burning
                    mouth
                    surcease
Lust is for a time
but the time for you
  is thyme for me.

1959

TO STRUM OLE HOMER'S LUTE

muse
    lemme hear
'bout that much disputed man
who upon felling Troy
                took to sea
        touching many lands
                sights & wonders
told & retold
            a hundred fold
abt his comrades folly
                as ref. their eating
Hyperion's herd
                    (& they were warnd)
thus went they to their doom;
Sing if you must
            begin
                    anyplace
        I hang upon yr lips

SONG OF MYSELF

this man who wants to hire me
   knows I'm a Poet

he does it out of sheer boredom
there is nothing between us.
his wife & children
                  strangers
he takes long rides alone in the car
                    bored w/ t.v.
Well, I know what you're thinking
    behind yr comfortable *intellectus*
& besides he is too old for all that

this man who wants to hire me
    & knows I'm a Poet

1965

LOVE, THE POEM, THE SEA & OTHER PIECES EXAMINED BY ME

... not so much for receiving

stolen goods

as for placing the junk

dead as the world

before the senses

In such times

one is put upon within

You know how we squeeze today

for meaning

the few words we have left to us

Here in a word is the sea before me

but the sea cannot be squeezed

So I sit as close to it as close as safe

The sea speaks if speech be sound

but speech is not sound

so turns for meaning

to the Poem

If the sea is anything

it is deep in silence

below

and beyond a few pebbles

chatter thrown against sand

Thalassa

the Greek reminds us

but the Greeks are profound and too

elude us and no one likes

to be found out.

In a dead world

as matter of course

California becomes a sun symbol

I supposed you

born there

So in thought I leap

thinking to rush up gladly

to greet you

just as would any

another creeping thing.

Along Washington St.,

the stores will close in an hour

—the sparrows are hopping about the grass by

to say its green I suppose and alive

with parasites I do not see

being birds these things do interest or they do not
                    they are still birds
                        —Saint Francis, indeed
              you were a fool
                        for had/not you
          we would all of us go screaming mad
                                    down the street so
              serious we are come to take ourselves.
Love, we say
                    but the flower we see
A Rose edges by degrees
          the secret locked tight within the unfold of bud
            the hedge that is the sea defines its limits.
In life
                Love
                        that switch/blade belly thrust
                          be quick
say what you will death is slowly
  withdrawing the blade of life
                        also Love
if in life I am ever in Love I am consumed.
                                    Choice?
              I shall
                    with doubt
                              bloom in my season
                    and bloomed
                        be blown out to sea
                                    or up
                    where the other gas,
      Heaven?
                    that is to come
                        in the Hollywood
                          of the end!
          But we have before tasted
                          those ecstasies of extreme unction
              so let's you and me
                          keep it clean and simple
                    complexity
                          not to be involved.
Poem is the child's ear
                    and love is naked and unashamed
              to cry that it is not fondled.
This reminds me
              that is the sea crys

                              its cry is
                    merely a surface noise.
Its secret is much deeper
                         but men are no longer interested
In the sea of their minds
                       they have visions of other worlds
       accurately numbered
                      they visit them daily in papers
                      and in the meantime plan
                         within a decade
                                      to shoot The Moon.

Good
                    as it is
          a dead issue in this they at least show foresight
Let them get out of the world
                          whatever means they may
          not by any long shot
                       is the sea dismissed from the mind
For a time the sea defines
                         the mind's periphery
          but after a time the sea is all around you
                         and over their worlds.
When you speak of
                    B. Donahue I think always the Irish Sea
                    his horses are also the sea's
          'tho we do bet our hard to come by
                         resources of life
                    the sea takes us
                                   horse and rider

                    In every race
It must be thus and so
                    Tragedy enters our lives
                    not so much B.
                                   Donahue as the Greek
          who also had notions of other worlds
          but continued to live by the sea
             as their language (which I have had of records)
                                           attest.

Today science fiction
                    yes but the real sea
          throwing hints as pieces of driftwood
                         the twisted gray remains
                    burn or preserve as what-nots
                              they give warmth or they give chill.

Mike, I have seen pieces of driftwood
                                    two
                        so twisted together you and I
                would be hard put to extricate. How can I so
                            subject our two lives to so trivial a thing
                    a twisted freak thrown together in the sea of
                        unconcern to be dis-
carded on some obscure beachhead of our world?
It is fat summer here and the ducks
                                    quack because of it.
    The birds will no longer come
                                to investigate the grass.   They
                work by signals
                                as we poor things pour
        over our signs for some parasite of meaning.
    It has been a lean season for you and me.
I did not intend a serious poem but the Poem
                        has a will all its own
I am a poor vehicle
                    a transport in summer were
I to be discarded also
                    in the season of decline.
            Love
                O self willed love
        though unworthy
                remember me kindly at the hour of decline
        know that I sacrificed all
                                to say nothing.
Hereafter
        it will be stark winter
                                every sign indicates it
In the long night there will be time enuf
To think what pigs we have made of ourselves.

ONE OF THREE MUSICIANS

The first time I heard Ornette
Coleman I thought
about Picasso's
                    Three Musicians
                    w/ their neo-
                        classical in-
struments: cigarboxes w/
                    soft line strains drawn
across barrel staves, tin

                            cans thrown
(or kicked) in Congo Square
                                these "fakers"
with jaw bone percussions out of dead
        horses & instruments from
                    the child's hand
They reproduce the spears, the screams
the outbursts of dark religious ex-
            orcisms. these are not the
shoed peasant feet out of Brueghel's
            painting *The Kermess*, these are
bare black feet pounding
                        delta clay
            the wire & steel singing over
                        broken barrel staves,
saying a theatre is any place
                    free associates come in
to play.

1961

FOR LEROI JONES

maybe that "quest thing"
could be "tightened" maybe
my things "have changed too"
maybe   lot-of-things
Like now you take out back here:
2 girls bounce ball
against a brickwall avoiding
the scrawl'd to the right of
            white perpendicular
                "F
                O
                U
                L"-line.

1960

A PROPOSITION (for Ed Marshall)

the true church
                    depends upon the ether
there are gods in the
          solemn air
          it is an triangular
                              affair
the altar: two stones
          support a third
                         a lintel beam
there is no roof
          for here the sun
                         is worshipped
          and by night the moon
with rememberd light
          comforts the howl
                         of worshippers and
other crawling lusts
Nor have we fared better
          in this common light that
                              made notoriously
                              reasonable
this most unhappy lot
          chance and
                         circumstance turns
all to stone and
          metallic purpose
                         sets no sights to move
or images to dance
          in streets that
                         machinery dismantled
departing have
          left the scene
                         to abstractions
of passions too

                    powerful to be
                              believed
                                        or if believed
too long endured
          what is partaken
                              is broken into fragments
without connection
          between the acts
                              things fall apart
"ananke prevails"
          the center does not hold
                              there is no return
what has been
          surrenderd
                              cannot be (re)claimed
the magic word
          has been lost
                              or if recalled
the parched
          tongue will not
                              articulate
terror issues from
          the deep
                              this is the first
                    day and nothing is
                                        to be done
for at the time
          I had not form
                    the wolf-dog
                              bayd at the foot
of the tower
          lacking the living voice

1961

AN ODE FOR GARCIA LORCA

In New Orleans Walt Whitman was married.
An Anglican priest duly performed the dark rite.
sub rosa. The Mint paid. So did the Butterflies
    and Lesbian Sparrows. (coined from old metal)
The Ceremony took place—slowly—in the shade!
Creole ladies avoided the sun like the plague.
'cadjuns', being the only pure stock,
                farmed their boys out like studs.
These are Walt Whitman's children. And here,
to convince you, is a photograph. A dirty
photograph. Beneath huey long's bridge,
    the which consumed ten hershey bars; The Pair
stripped to the waist, standing in drains:
The Sun upon their belly buttons. Outsized,
(these pictures always exaggerate) low hanging cloud for
        adjective.
The bride's maid, with a bunch of pansies, (fades) were
        graciously received. There are no differences here!
There are also his children and, in case I didnt warn you,
this is a poem.
The background is a blurr about the horizon.
NOTE: In a photograph the foreground is by that time
        background, (adding "not really" to it).
            It's five O'clock.
            It gets dark early.
            I cant see to finish this.

ORNITHIC SCENE

these pigeons,
                    when
                              no bread is thrown them,
repair to this,
                    half dead from the top,
ailanthus tree;
                         discussing among themselves
          those things
                              pigeons are concern'd to:
avant garde fare
                    (from Paris, mainly
a rehash'd up to us at home, decades later)
                         aviary lore
confronting the "new"
                              music
                                   mostly from the below
living branches full of
                         sparrows
pulling off 'sit-ins' as it were
                    & w/ strident catcalls
     to the new philistines
       the all of which
                              is to send the cats
against that brickwall
                         beyond whose rhetoric
they may not go.

1964

from EXERCISES FOR EAR

I

in trips sweet may
upon those damsel
feet of hers

carpets spreading
green before her
cowslip & clover

down to banks of
ever chuckling streams
of gurgle-happy

waters & the sky
's one big squash
of pumpkin smile

III

in this same parc
I saw, broad as day,

two sailors take
turns in the eighth

geodetic year of
getting to know

earth-mother while
two chapters bodily

lifted themselves from
the King James

version
of thou shalt nots

IV

Poets barred
from Plato's utopia
take pleasure in yr
derision

those immutable laws
that formalized the

egyptian into
stark rigidity can

never harden into
the arteries of yr things

V

in summer when
the women
put their hair up

sitting in pairs
in this parc
or they ply

perambulators thru
wearing shorts
or in slacks

yaking the yak-yak
women yak   this
I also love

IX

. . . too
there is the preacher
who ev'ry
sunday

pushes junk to

his conger-
gation but
just you let
me try for kicks
and don't

the man come
bustin' my door
        in saying

        i'm wrong

X

a hollow
        victory

you celebrate
bird singing alone
in this cold

XII

in america
            the rich
are poor &

            the poor
outraged
        since no

peasant tra-
            dition
to lend

        dig-
nity to cheap-
            ness

XIV
(*epitaph*)

it's to my late
departed friend I owe
a word more a
         line or two: yr

works I disposed of
               had to

fuzz you kno
tho' pages of blanks,

the tablet I
keep cal-

ligraphers' de-
                  light

Rest In Peace

XVI

how
muthafucker
                  am I

'spose to hear
     a fuckin'
                  muse

if you keep
          on
          talkin'/

XVIII

ya been tellin'
me lies
          all along

the which
          i be-
lieved

     along w/
that shock
          of blond

hair
     in & about
yr twat

          of late
tightly closed
               to me

XIX

Echo, a beautiful nymph
     loved the woodland sports

          tho' favord of Diana,
she had one fault:

                    she talkd
too much

     the rest
needs no repeating

XX

the world which
     promises
               so much
tho' short on delivery
          but never
                    the
syndrome of
               politicating
adenoids via the radio

& christ yes
                the T.V.!

XXII

the nymph Clytie so
            enamoured of Apollo

she followed his move-
                ments

                        like radar
and she,

            imagine it,
just another flower

XXIII

. . . and Minerva there
            arm' d to the teeth
sprang

            plumb bang
from the center
                of his

ole Zeus' mind
            (Hermes perhaps by
as midwife, t'attest)

                    so trans-
ported were they who
    grew heroes out of

                    trees

XXIV

love comes
    in an eye-
           dropper

w/ afixd
        sort of
             spike

to the ele-
        vation & the

e-

    mendation of
           the few

XXVI
        (por Andrew Crozier)

when the old
measure's gone

     & the new
stresses feet

tho' the heart
    stagger & the head

be still
       let the feet go

        black & bare
      let 'em go

         black & bare
       let 'em go

          & etc.

XXVIII

being of unsure mind
        & shaky morals
he betook himself

           to be first
a butterfly then something
approaching a hot dog

alas, he married into money
& as is to be anticipated
        has sired

a whole
        pocketful
        of small change

XXIX

        (dian)

the Moon
      that is not hell bent
on coming in

        atop
the window ledge
           has turned lopsidely

the other cheek
         to let fall
darkly   its crescent arch

XXX

europe wrecked
     america w/o signposts:

adrift, a gigantic flotilla
amassd   all the fires
of the old Hells

                    plus potential of

ultra-high explosive
                    & all mannd by

small letters
          sans punctuation

XXXIII

i try to get on
w/ people

               they owe me
i don't or

it's the wrong size
& i oversleep

put me back
          two days   look

   & i'll catch you
saturday

               great

XXXIV

thinking in verse
to avoid
          the medi-
ocre   i omit
                    yr things
but here

               in a yester-
day antholo-
               gy

               here
you come to-
          day

XXXV

a musick
a spreck
  a formal rack-
    et in time

a yak-yak
  a means
  of talkin' back

XXXVI

it's to dave brubeck
i initially
   owe

three short bars
  sans musical no-
    tation

that the horn player,
shinin' thru,
   deciphers

XXXVII

don't as rule
trample underfoot
   the serpent

wrapd aroun' my staff
  aesculapus-wise.
    meal consumed

returned to invisible watchings
(seken)
  not meticulous of habit

at times rather long-
  winded:
   a.

the things i know
                    b. things i hate
w/ reserve of venom

                    to those
to whom it applies   sum: proper man
over & above this

                    a watchful eye
to that horde of golden apples
the which acquired only afta

            herculean
                    whuch-a-ma-trials

XXXVIII

if on towards
                    the end of summer
i forgetting to cross my knees
        where fewer leaves

cover upper reachers
where my b.v.d.'s etc.
                    lament not
there is always that higher

needing not fig evergreen
                            or yew
to hide from meaner eyes
                            than those

my god
            i pray you take
the lofty
                view

XXXIX

meeting you
            & afta all these years
in a supermarket

what joy with yr approach

            background'd jars & tins
                        of labeld invites
greens & reds the
                        entire spectrum

me the while among the cheeses
                        & oleo's
how nice to see you

                        & a dozen eggs

XLI

yr non-essential be-
                havior reawakens
darkly   the old gods within:

phallic sportings
                        cleftd-footed revels
of scrawld
                indigations
                                on walls
of men's rooms

XLII

fabulous being several parts
    of four animals
                        blessd w/ wings
& silence
                to keep watch over meaning
i suppose under-
                        standing

& esoteric tradition
                united or separated
you embrace
                the four corners
                        of heaven

XLIII

that xmas Tom
when you like

took all the bread
split & goofd

it all on
        stuff & there

was Jan screaming
like in free

        verse for
Lar's tree &

santa claus
        for the twins

man like it
        hits me now
what she sd:
it's always this way

XLV

there've been
        so many poems
i can't remember
                them all:

the bright ones
                w/ fair hair
strident intellects
        eyes dark & keen

the minor ones
        turnd in as if
to retreat from life
        oh there are bad poems

so let us record the fact

XLVII

    ev'ry day
bam-a-lam-a-lam

& the sun comes shinin' up
'n somebody makes it

    new   minted half-dollar
                 sixty-fo'

J.F.K. in profile

        E.
     B.   R.
   I.   T.
  L.   Y.
        fer halo
"hallelujah"
          (the amen corner

XLVIII

once next door
      there was

a large
    family

grandparents
      two or three children
   their
      husbands &

wives the
    familial din
was terrific
      but

they sold the damn
    place & moved
  on to suburbia
        some-

how it's not the same
        the house
given over
            to

apartments
                roomers
coming & going
            on the street

we never speak
        transients
                    they

may be any-
            thing.

L

i seldom go
    to beacon hill
any-

        more to
peep in at
        louieburg sq.

where time
            has propted up
the old trees
& the brick
        of the houses
not unlike

            that shade
of t'ang
            terra cottas

before buddha
                    in-
vaded the
            central
province

                    w/ too much

of ev'ry-thing
                    for my taste

    LI

this misdemeanor
            which sur-
                        vived

(due to medico-
            techno-
                        logical

know-how) was bred
in a movie
                    of a mind

that's a
            patchwork
of comic

                    books
from a
            mortality

that slides out
    from under-
                        neath

    LV

refine yr vices
separate
            the dross

            &
they'll dig up
yr mss.

two thousand

            years late
like they

        wuz dead
sea
        scrolls

LX

. . . for all its tawdry cheapness
        the religious scapulas,
                    printed sentiments

of gone novenas   the too too
    preciosos of saviours w/thorns
                joe dunn used to

bring in to me from charlestown;
he knew, tho' never spoke,
        preferring bob creeley's

things   he was
            an oasis among this
desert of irish sand

LXI

like my jazz
        low-down
& my blues mutha-
            huckin'
                    dir-
                        ty
now don't chu' go
            'N blow no whistle
        on me 'cause
i'll tell the man
        all ya biz'ness
this i got from
            miz mess
        hoodsie-cap's
                in her horn

where she-it she keeps
                    her stash

LXII

"i want you to get
  dressed-up in your
        s.s. uniform and pretend
i'm a pris'ner of war and
  then ask me questions i
can' possibly answer
                    i want you to
call in your friends and
        have them stand aroun'
and call me filthy names
      you can take me with you
i'll be your slave . . ."

LXIII

tho' my songs
    not deckd out in
baroque trimmings
        of adjective baubles
they, nonetheless, stand
        lean & cleanly de-
fined against a gray de-
                cember sky
as against the on-coming
        of a spring
when all shall be
                too gaudily dis-
playd   w/ too much of ev'
            rything to be
clearly outlined

LXIV
        (por G.L.)

the set-up of a poem
    may not always please

the eye;
            but the ear can be
led
        conducted along
                surprising causeways
where the hither-to un-
                            expected
        (one might even venture un-
suspected)
                comes in-
                        to prominence.
the tongue whetted
                to taste (not
forbidden
                that's too categoric)
cautioned against/
                have i connected?

LXV

. . . blues aint nuthin'
    but which gender you
makin' it w'th
                split

& you want
        some-body to
please come hear
        & gimme sum'um
this *mornin'*
                —don't call no
doktor 'cause he
        cant do'me no good

                lord-lord
                            lord
jus'
        gimme sum'um

    'cause i doan' kere

LXVII

Fetching   yes levi tights sad-
dle shoes   swim thru fuck-
   ing streets   men in yr wake

saliva eyed your comely ass
biting words of outraged women
pursue you thru

cheap hotels contemptible rooming
houses   loose yr petals till
the bare stamen   then come to me

we'll read Hart Crane together
D.H. Lawrence, the unruly, or
H.D.   fittingly to assuage you

LXVIII

cars zip past   fart & growl
at intersections   streets of
anonymous alcoholics   innocent

pickpockets hot angels cruising
the crucified streets   burning
        outsized lampbulbs

illuminating nothing   save it be
the gutter   ghosts of freud
the deadliness of you

LXIX

placid at evening
sky's clear   cloud bank to north

season's year; head infusing tail
    wind's a feather's wisp   Moon

in Her final resolve   stars arrange
    themselves in choir stalls

cantata of skylights   roofs
       & chimney pots

LXXIV

Tony, your head is for
       dark kisses; it is
the rear'd heads of stallions
charging across fragments of

Edison Marbles, it is the
       Minotaur conquer'd by Love
of indeterminate sex; it is also
for secret thots of poets & their

profane proclivities & so it is
that i stand erect *ecce homo*
   behold the male lust!
(thus, do i think of you, mi luv,
      afar O wld that i were
all Silver backing the mirror
(full length) & cld see you
     barely
           whole in the nude!

LXXVII

lament lament
      the liquidation of the rose
& the passing of our lilly

yr june is over & all yr
      beauties sleep
plow'd under

        your sacred close
all yr petal'd blossoms
         to dust

lament lament
      the liquidation of the rose
& the passing of our lilly

Poet whose joy

        whose love it was
to dote on you
        long since turn'd

to other spheres, their metric's
        another tune
lament lament
    the etc. of the rose
& so on of our lilly

LXXIX

what has been for me
  a lifetime of watching how
things go is to you nothin'
      better to do
but then you take your values
as you take your gage

happy in my segregation
    i hoot at passing cars
& hope w/ all my heart
  to spot me
        a bird or two

LXXX

  the poem comes most of
    the time mid-first then

aft the first ass backwards
  but the music! ah, that cues
me   a w/o which yr pro-
     gressions wld not find
& so forth to end of that theme

wldn't you know & o the wjo
    a too liberal allowance
        fer individual
dif'rences of
     what else but
imaginative discourse

LXXXII

the great maimd selecting one of
its own to lord it over 'em

another four years   the last election
was the sow's entrails served up

to "the people" on a chaffing dish.
the non-existent issues   the in-

cumbent administration's abuse of
power   their control of communication

media. it was as always "the people"
who lost an election:

scraps thrown to the various nationality
groups of dogs irrespectrive of

markings. maimd & broken heirs of the
little Republic

                that got busted
                all because . . . etc & on

LXXXIV

. . . nor, in this common light, have we
                fared better, most
  unhappy lot
                made no-
                        toriously reasonable;
chance and circumstance turns all to
                cold metallic purpose
setting no sights to move or to dance
the image, dismantled
                        all that machinery
                                departed,
leaving the scene to
                maudlin abstractions,
                        passions too powerful to be believed
or if believed,
                too long endured

LXXXV

in the age of frescoes he
                married the classic image
adding to it his own
                        outraged agonies
        depending from the lower limb
            of some Paduan master;
the vulture surveys almost the entire can-
                vas. so one thinks of
                        Chagall's husband floating past,
caught-
        up in a swirl
                        of past regrets. it is
an audacious willingness to experience

LXXXVI

long before the first
            robin comes
                        the girl upstairs
does
        it's that old inner
                spring   of hers
that maketh me
                    to sit up
    & take note

LXXXIX

take my hand
        o gentle christ
& lead me to
        the boneyard

where amidst an
        erudition of stoned
compatriots
                i'll wear
tradition out

take my hand

o gentle christ
& lead me to
the boneyard

my will is simple:
not to be longwinded
concerning things
short as life

take my hand
o gentle christ
etc.

XCII
(J.F.K.)

year afta the hero
struck a blow to our
bourgeois sentiments
—what he sd
for then what has a president
to do w/ overt acts
hamstrung as the Poet . . .
(he was warm to human re-
dundancy   that
& a strong aroma of lilacs

XCIV

ah would that
life were the long-
est side Getz
ever cut & Death
an ex-
tended play

XCV

so it is w/ the return
of another spring
La Primavera & Botticellian

spray as a shower of gold;

afta the dead season
        thinking to have lost
my   voice   til
            bud by bud
the Poem unfolds
          itself

then the flower
     at the top-most
   that will be the title

   each fruit smacks
       of its own savour
no two Poems alike

XCVIII

. . . nation's purse strings handed over
     cum gratis
        & in *toto* to a banking fraternity
of money grubbers; upon some such
       sentiment of folly
          does their slime de-
pend; pitifully funded
       —& sold the Republic for a piece of chit,
for a rattle of tin cans
      yea, even a box of twisted wires.
this is one Hell you won't
      legislate easily
        yr way out of

XCIX

a line of thot pull'd
  across the narrow page
    precipitating thot
intoning vowel sounds

lend moderation to the pro-
gressing subterfuge

found in the Viaticum
of Agony; Mantegna   trans-

form'd the dead Christ in-
  to a foreshorten'd
        dwarf. the heavy
marble renders an erie

  glow but the hollow
O's of human woe are ev'
    ry where pro-

nounced lend-
        ing no en-
couragement to the
   "afta the fact"

C

having read
      Homer
        Ovid
          & Shaxspeare
(each in his own tongue)
         he thot that he wld
do us an επος;
            strange figures
   that emerge
        from a landscape
heretofore
     strangely still

CII

at "that place" in Cambridge (Mass.)
  that Mr. John Adams de-
            clined to teach
& are caught up w/ ev'ry craze
    as pandemonium above a drone of squares,
     so on a clear day
       the text-books are audible
         So That

you cannot breathe   to tell
whether pupil or pedagogue it bee

th' gaff'n the gass ov it
            to threat'n us as it were
t'other side the Charles
                        with "poetry"
nothin' seems much less likely
            save for a few trial balloons
no Homer has come

because of that smog
                        & so forth . . .

CIV

you are doll under
        some vague aroma
                that i (for some say culi-

                                nary purpose)
yr not so heavenly (   )
nothing cld be further a-
            field of my o-
                        riginal
                    gambetto
letz say drop it the huh
                subject easily as you
do yr pantz
            tiens

CV

i write poetry be-
        cause of
(non-separation of the
    men from the animals)
            the in parenthesis
        found common ends
so combined forces
            to oh anything
                    hurray
            you name it

152

extinguish The Sun!

& go next door
       where cummings put you
on to a swingeroo of a
       new universe!

go go GO

CVI

"man doan chU no
  der chink'z
      gonna blast U
    'n ever-
         body else
who aint chink
    write off'fin ther
fase ov ther (no longer
        God's green) earth
when they git enuff
    guided missles
        T'accomplish
the feat
     (hey,
        waitaminette
        ahm kullood tu"

CVII

if eveebodeEz sew
      awl-fieD Eqwaal
how-cum cho(pee) bloak's got
    forty billyun scalps
       (termd dollars) in eye

  aint got
      price ah cuppa koffee
the which (by the time i gitzit)
      gone up to
        fifteen seentz, Huh
answer me thaT

                    mistir might-as-well-bee
        computer
                    and you kan jus' kool-it
on th' poeTREE the which you
            can save fer henry jones
                'cause he doan
                    eat noe greek

CVIII

    i have come to
chew up yr language

to make more palatable
the L's & collaterals

            (at the service
                entrance

CIX

arrived today from one story st.,
"that place across the river," again their new

from the bindery H advocate
        the which containd some old WCW, until

when suppressed; Pound & some by the grace
ov god, the goode dr. Eliot, Schlesinger

(the upstart) & the two Roosevelts, teddy
& whoosie—unholy marriage in common & all

to i suppose say now it can be told.
they sit on a man's mss until he'

    s dead so's they can make sure he's em-
balmed before they publish him. they oughtta

pass over that pile of classic brick w/a sleeping
spray & put it out 'ov its misery.

CXII

yr Litle World surrounded w/
    newsprint, maintain'd in orbit
via artificial improvisation a
pink innoculated soul

peeks out onto the sani-
                tary landscape where
abstract cars fart carbon Sums
to chase the split-person'd

Artist thru & under sluice-jazz-
ways in rapid transits screaming:
don't just take these
            words from me

CXV

on towards the end of
    summer when God created
ev'rything & said nothin'
    you fall in the pad
            poppin' yr fingers
    callin' ev'rybody "baby"
(i dug the works on yr hip
        & eyes for fixin' up
in my kitchen

CXVII

once i saw Bird so high
        that he came wingin'
over from the apple
w/ a busted foot & a gig
        to make at roll-a-way
he came in on the chorus
        from a wheelchair &
    just made the bridge
on one wheel
                oh, man the hippies
at mass. & columbus

were moderately
shook!

CXVIII

& there was "Pres"
   horn horizontal aslant
      blowing nothin' but
      free verse
& all them jitterbugs
   outta' their skulls
         on B's flyin'
from the second balcony
the while cool hippies lookd on
      in *gran dispétto*

CXX

in time of war
      it must be
tough on birds
   who can neither
            a-
light nor come
         to nest,
taking no sides
      (inter-
            jurisdictional,
                        eh)
like the mind
            they hope
to rise above it
i wish i were
   a bird & not
      held-down to
anything in par-
         ticular
oh, you name it

CXXI

oh fertile brain
you will never cease
to be a sore spot
of introspective
contention
finding answers to questions
you can't even come up with

CXXIV

this what
    has an ass's
which's not
screwd on

    properly
& caught up
is he by ev'
ry craze
        up-
shot con-
    siders 'im-
self on parlance

w/ avant-garde
what question
    mark IS happ'
ninGs.

        some satis-
faction over
    this herd of
credulity

        rests
upon him
        light-
            ly

CXXV

reverend Dr. Eliot
exit'd, e.e.
        gone; Dr.
Pound in his dotage

    well, there's
Henry
        (Miller, that is)
who keeps right on
        talking
            to The Wall
like he was a Sephardic jew
& the diaspora
    a coming
        attraction

CXXVI

write yr things w/ care & pre-
    cision   in extreme emergency
blunt pencil cue you; an erasure be
yr salvation;

            but then you are bent
on putting people on:
                    fastidious;
            unknowing

but hell bent on
        appearing as tho' you did.
hard to maintain consistency in these
ways.   dont dare make

            a prediction as to
how you'll end up. hit 'im ovah the head
w/ a stick 'cause he aint playing right?
    or softer

        shaking yr head in 'fuddled
bepuzzlement tho' careful to maintain yr
safe distance for may do anything

Nota:

goes w/ out saying
you have search'd yr own insides for
similar
            wrong-way-ons

CXXVIII

it is the Extraction, Fermentation
    & Distillation of the Vine
fruit that upon drinking
            the sedation sol fa ti do
& mayhaps the Alchemical
                        Marriage
or the Mind's heady brew . . .

CXXXI

just broke
    outta' re-
form school
        w/ two
other harden'd
emigrunts

    & all
w/ eyes for
    coolin' it

in my pad
    that is clean
but

        far from cool

CXXXV

O woman who will never kno
the taste of angelic gissom
for her husband's always juiced

so's too peter'd out to get it
up let 'er lone spiel into that
screwd up pan she calls

a face, swinburnian protestations
of lyrical cuss words among a
clatter of yesterday's pots & pans

unwashéd for music & poetry is all
their celtic delight or sicilian
nights (back to back in the leveling

bed) the syracusian dionysius,
faunus & priapus & all their train
denied those parts that men delight

                    to see

CXXXVI

i would drink the poppy's juice
had i the price or climb mt. everest to e-
jaculate its pointed crest, loose my sperm
in the rarified upper air

wrestle The Four Beastes, ascertain what sex
& blow their trumpet of The Judgement Day, turn
on The Sun & Moon, send them doin' the twist
juice up The World til The Lady (tipsy) tottles

loosing her scarf hiding her nakedness from
meaner viewers—this veil's no cover for modesty
for in things higher the shew is to the quick
& no word can expose what word expose

a fire burns within my Temple see how the tongue
licking the element's assholes my eyes burn
& my mind stuff leaps up to my God, Glory be
the centerped, a million angels beat their wings

orgasm their gissom explode in celebration
                    abt the God-head.

CXXXVII

the nigger
ought to be
    horse-

whipd
for his
presumptions
but, my friend,

when i look a-
  bout me at
this emi-

  grunt dis-
order that passes
for White

i'm inclined to
      a-
        gree

CXXXVIII

when i consider how my nights are spent
yea, in my skull & out, there is no
sin but ignorance, my good Marlowe hath

sd. (but yours somehow detaches you from
the sullen herd, for i have slept between
yr thighs hunger & thirst you satis-

fied. what if anything do you read? you
left me, badly framed, an old dutch mas-
ter's print facing an empty bed in which

    nobody sleeps

CXLI

compared to Walt Whitman
ginsberg wins by a nose
in a harlem where they are
selling defective grease-paint
to the mulattoes   but in Hayte
where they black-ball their sun-

tans tho' the rigmarole of the
fact finding boards lend little
credence to their efforts

               against the sun

CLIV

to write well was all
     i ever wanted, really
& now that i may do so i've no
          other ambitions: save, be it,

to on occasion go up to Cape Anne
     along Annisquam river to in-
spect the briar rose for a trace of
          salt or to climb

the back of "portegee hill" for a
peep in at Our Lady of *bon viaje;*
     or out to Pigeon Cove w/ yclept
of "the tough one" caught

                    in the unstopt ear,
full-faced, into the bite
               of the salt wind

CLV

when the man
     blows his saxophone
we listen
          as to a poet

speaking of his a-
        bandon'd or
     slower, in a lower
octave, speaks of this
        everlasting
           enigma

CLVII

most of th'noise
     out of the village
& no. beach
       are promissary notes
in default (seeing not

they can't deliver the
     goods
          why don't they
just get off the pot?
       (at that,
the lot of 'em squat
     to piss
         or shld,
anyways

CLXI

oh america
     Egypt tried yr folly
& faild, miserably
 (circa   XXth Dynasty)
           because of an
excess importation of
     charcoal via the
       White Nile;
the Assyrian swept in
     shutting off the e-
lectricity to
     the κιθλρλ
          amplifier

CLXV

in love's immediacy all my fond
                    cares move
quietly out to sea

                              as i am caught
up in a veritable laocoon
                    of convoluted in-

volvements. having no sons i alone
surrender to hate's
                    arch enemy

& my sighs of woe
                              are heard
              in that place

CLXVIII

his'try, the which contains
              more time & less space w/
no action to speak of;
                              a mere super-

station like clothing metaphores;
God, i wld rather run naked
    thru the beginning askance in
Genesis like an Abanza tribesman

high as Euclid
                        wearing nought but
smiles to say it's
all good & still swinging

CLXXII

the apple,
              which did not fall,
remains
              after the incidents
it aroused, to reinforce the

                    concrete &
whose cross-
                    section scientists find
still in-
          tact the perfect sym-
bol of symmetry & geo-
                    metric harmony

CHORALE AND HYMN

IV

CHORUS invocation key sentiment in the manner of the north american pop
ballad—searching after the manner of Blue Miles number to close in on a
jubilant choral hymn shouted as would a congregation of american 'nigger'
foot washers.

          Waters the Centaur the
Blue horsemen some
               men are
       born to horns.
  I waited for you the
             Bridge the
                 Cranes from
      all over America
             'Round about Midnite'
     waited
        and still
           waited by who
               frames the
picture who
      the great
          Blue Miles.
(queens are
      lonely not so
           people have escape hatches) the
    reaches of the Blue
          Painter who so loved
           his waters engulfed
he became as Narcissus
         love the
          waters of compassion
     engulfed him. Stay
         bearded
       boy with Lars climbing
     in windows (shit
        if I didnt have to
    go first and know
         so fucking much
        we - - -)
    now I think back - - - Echo
          the Cranes.

From
          the Bridge to
      the broken span and now
          comes the failure of the Poem as
    a Reconstructed
                      Disconnection

                    V

HYMN

      Waters
              now with fish out you
return with your
              jig habit your
                      junkie ways of

    neo-
        classical "soft line strain"
with boy talk and other
                  fly blown trivia your
      innocence raises you to
                          become a testament to dirt
Come junkies   perverts
        boosters pimps prostitutes
        you hip tossers shakers you
        who mount horsemen barebacked
                  you wops you hunkies you
        kikes spicks frogs you
brits   chinks   Come
              form your coronal creeps
      from under all the caves and seas of the old world
              yes and you tar
                          and ward heelers too   red
      necks   panhandlers arrested elizabethans
                  from behind the smokies
          Come join in ye coronal
to her belly roll
                  resound her red rock and
roll the notes
              pure and real
              and you reds turned
pink from wallowing high church names
          behind the foothills

                    167

maniacs   fathers making it
                              upon sons and daughters
                with brothers snakes
                                  and their handlers   goofers
        licking balls sniffing coke you
                          purists who pop rollers et
non sequiturs   ALL COME
                      hymnal to her boobies
black and blue all
                              all of you Motherfuckers
shout it loud and let the wound on her couch
            circle about the mystic youths the finest to
throw themselves upon spikes to her service
        cover the secret of flowers

VI

POSTLUDE

The poet is a lonely queen
                              the ace jester stabbed or restrained
                by the conspiracy in the Privy
                            as to my knight errant:

                                                  stabbed in the night
                            in his back
                                    they lodged
                          swords
                I have not consulted my cards since)
        With my dog tag
                        "The Hanged Man" I go in
            the night among my horsemen (my cavaliers)
                    boosters, horsemen (are unicorns) busted fairies
                their lovers (tho mostly duds) such as is
                              my Coffee House
                    my Boswell Wieners   whose
                    tape recorder Measure

                                          the word
                                          heaven . . . .

168

              our sessions in the souterraine place
          where the Dragon spikes his tail
            assemble in limbo a few musicians to
make

                 a combo   we sit in
                     to dig the sounds . . . .

UNPUBLISHED WORK

THE ENIGMA

being of unsure mind
        and shaky morals
    he betook himself
        to be first a butterfly
something approaching a hot dog
    alas he met his doom
    in a saloon w/a leaky gaspipe
lacking virtue
    he married into money
and as to be expected
        has sired a whole
        pocketful of small
                change

MANIFESTO

. . . in some ways you do
          frankly astound me
now you take timmy
that's the next door cat
four puffs of white feet
          pads up and down
thru the dead leaves
  stop a little here a
    little there to poke his
nose under then pounce
                to send the pigeons by
      to a great scurry of wing flaps
they take to the naked
          branches above
                what could he find
there to interest him so?
I remember the area
          from last summer,—
                    bare as a bone's ass
save for spots of grass
          and tree root humps
from beneath

                    —back to the greeks
who like the Freudians
    had a word for
                        everything and as Gertrude
Stein noted: we do like
      to call names.   no
                    I want to be free
      uncategorized   the—
x factor   the elusive   neutron
      not to be tagd and
shut between musty volumes
        on the shelves above
the heads of bookworms
          read but not quite "QUICK
        the door" door halfclosed
            he makes it
the train (his) is waiting
      I continue as I was

Winter 1964

174

THE MOON IS NUMBER 18

the youth of my
    generation re-
paird

      to the Moon
thither did their senti-
         ments piti-

fully meet.
        broken phrases
that grope

       in the half
light

Summer 1965

SPHINX

fabulous being
        several parts
of four animals
          blessed with wings
& silence
            to keep watch over meaning
                I suppose
                        understanding
& Esoteric tradition
          united or separated
you embrace
            the four corners
of Heaven

August 1965

A FANTASY

in time of war
   it must be
tough on birds

who can neither
        alight
nor come to nest

like the mind
   (interjurisdictional)
      taking no sides

they hope to rise
      above it;
I wish I were

       a bird
not held down to
anything in particular

June 1965

POST MORTUM P.S.

walk w/a lightfoot
              you above ground
knew—slowly—that I too once
bestrode like a colossus

up & down that beckoning turf
              & in my day did
    grasp the light
& did Him wrestle

til the bell tolld
              the final round

Spring 1966

A CATALOGUE

The clean facks of my life
spread

      out upon this table-top be-
fore me: a
          new pack of cigarettes 2
          notebooks filed to ca-
pacity with
        other people's affairs
pair of gloves which,
            now that it's warm
and spring's up us I
          wont need, a
tarot pack, a
        red leather backed edition of
Leo Frobonius
        's the *Childhood of Man*, 2
keys that dont fit
         the new lock, an
empty bennie jar with 2
           dexadrines left
       in another (unseen). Good
I shall write tonite.

March 1961

THESE THINGS

    that come up to me

on the streets & I take 'em

      home where no one's

waiting save Penelope

        my jay-bird

who caws at me

           from atop her perch

of unlighted candle

        labeld red

overcomed I stuff

        her craw

w/ cornmeal mush

     & all to flutters

of happy wings

1965

IN PARTICULAR

tho' anatomy is not a butcher's knife
      one can use its keen edge to
                lop off
                        branches, out-croppins
on foreign trees.

Men take more delight in their rations
      (today) than in their
                  "head's following
the foot, in an orderly mode of"
—mode of word procedure. a-piece of word
                procedure.

"you sure do have strange looking feet"
from walking up and down on those
                heavenly streets.

"a T-squared thing to determine
      all things" 2. now rare.
3. Finance, (even more so)
          Genesis in the first place
is Rectification of *names*.

"Determine a precise terminology
          and no more fuss about it."
For a T-squared thing is
          a thing of supremacy, reigning over the
          dumb-founded as beastes and fowles
peoples the ayre.

more, it is the Law of Divine Right to pass
      the scepter pointing out an
          here things and a there thing rememberd.

Divine notable distance between
              these. prediction:

          Divine Magic
          between 3

Known Kings.
prediction
—of the 4th estate.

What creeps
in between the lines?

Sept '62

APHRODITE

when she with her old
        beauty arises
               rejuventated
from the sea   shed
          are all my old desires
& the waves lapping the edge of
      her peignoir

Summer 1965

ON THE COMMON

old codgers in their

    cool years sitting

it out on the hard benches

    of life   facing a

fountain that's not even

  connected & could

    care less.

Sept 1968

O A NUMBER I KNO

In the age of frescoes he
                 married the classic image
adding to/it his own
                              outraged agonies
                 depending from the lower limb
of some Paduan master.
The vulture surveys almost the entire can-
                 vas. So one thinks of
                 Chagall's husband floating past,
caught/up in a swirl
                              of past regrets. It is
an audacious willingness to experience.

IDYL

Priapus
      the garden deity
             guides us over this wall
      tho his cult is
          no longer ordaind
      his presence is
          nonetheless
still felt here
       among cyclamen, tulips
             & the rest
a bulbous thought
       in a season that is
            still early
he may yet bring
       fulfillment to
       all anxious lovers

Spring 1961

POEM

leaves are voices of
           children
           are they not too
                   leaves.
the excitement of their laughter
           like leaves
           moving together
   to no other purpose
           than this
           that they move
           laughingly.
the gamely sight
           of their lauighter
           provoking shade to
           light reflectors
           here and far now
           this way then
                   that
   —not chiaroscuro
                     no
   not as subtle as all that
           no tensile light dance
           this facing me
           tree with no leaves
invoking reversals.

1959

[UNTITLED]

i'm thinking
this cat

who has ev-rything
& sez nothin'

        (what'r you thinkin'
          about?)
o nothin' but

i'm thinking too
baby, this tune could

go on forever
what say you

    we keep it that way

WHAT CAN I TELL YOU

what can I tell you,
            since tell you I must
shall I hearken back
            to the pollution
                        of our rivers & streams
no, I rather think I had
                  better not.
the river is also the mind
            which, if we remember,
      is also a stream of consciousness.
            we who hug the shores,
                  near the points of our
            recent embarkations,
cannot know the horror
            repressed in the sub-
      sediments
                        here where the memory
      is received
                  into the sea,
            which refuses nothing.
we would do well,
            to hesitate   before
advancing into
  this hinterland
      where chaos has bedded
      with Night
                  and thrown up
      these monsters who
  so assault our dreams
that we cry out,
         at the apparition
      of that monster
            of gargantuan
                        proportions
  half awake or asleep
            but always desiring.
sea scum sucked in and out
  by the lipping tide
  we remember sea anemone
and the youth of effeminate ways

  doubly loved and enamored

                of his reflection
          anemone petals they are
          for memory
                        and the wine stains

IL SAGGIO

we are the noble

      & intelligent few

to understand love

      in the abstruse

Sept 1968

SPROUT BUT NOT FLOWER

. . . what has been for me
      a lifetime of watching how things go
is to you nothing better to do
but then you take your values
      as you take your gage

happy in my segregation
  I hoot at passing cars
and hope with all my heart
to spot me a bird or two.

April 1965

ARS MAGNA
Stephen Jonas, Initiate
1966

First Matter of the Work

essential qualities:
  a. love of God
  b. unselfishness
  c. charity
  d. detachment from earthly interests
        – including material wealth
        and dedication to eternal things

"is the work of the incorruptible Fire at an end?"
and answered: "the perfect gold has come from the Athanor."

. . . that Salt, Sulphur and Mercury seem to be
Spiritual principles; that the secret purpose
was to analyse, rectify, integrate, the human
spirit; and to produce the perfect man."
                                        A.E.W.

called also the "Hermetic Work," analagous to
"Spiritual Mysteries."

. . . that true Alchemia was a practice of
Divine Knowledge.
termed also Work of Philosophy.
"orange": of the glory of the world
"red" of his anger
blue-gray of formal calm

----

the supreme dream of the alchemists, the transmutation
of the weary heart into a weariless spirit – WBY
. . . all must be dissolved before the divine
substance, material gold or immaterial essences
awake.
our (alchemist's world is of immortal essences
"deep searchings" of Jacob Böhme, the Teutonic
Theosopher, on all things relative to God, man
and the universe. (not an alchemist) but
by ex hypothesi sua, attempted to
unfold the true nature of the Great Work and

the qualifications essential to its performance.
Note: reason for concealment or "veiling":
that the art might be misused by those
*greedy for power – perhaps – or par esempio
the Freudians + Jungians
*moreover: "There is no power to
attain unto it, unless a man first
become that himself which he seeketh
therein: no skill or art availeth.

Universal Tincture or Philosopher's Stone
"Turba" or "that which accomplishes the
anger of God"?! Jacob Böhme – this
is all taken – i.e. the above.

Böhme in his <u>Aurora</u> says that gold + silver
cannot be made "pure or fine" unless they
are "melted seven times in the fire"
when that is done gold or silver "remaineth
in the middle or central seat in the heart
of nature, which is the water, sitting in its
own quality and colour."
It's Böhme who first affirms that the
gift of alchemy is the spirit of supernatural
life and that the Stone is Christ – i.e.,
Christ the Spirit. "This is the noble
precious Stone – <u>Lapis</u> <u>Philosophorum</u> –
the Philosopher's Stone, which the magi
do find, which tinctureth Nature and
generateth a new son in the old."

A. It is at once manifest and hidden:
it is hidden in this world and yet
may be had everywhere.

Correspondences between Planets + metals
from inferior to superior: 7 capital sins

1. Saturn	lead	avarice
2. Jupiter	tin	greed
3. Mars	iron	wrath
4 Venus	copper (Hermaphrodite)	lust
5 Mercury	mercury	envy
6 Moon	silver (imagination)	sloth
7 Sun	gold (<u>word</u>)	pride

Apollo symbolizes the sun in its spiritual
aspect

----

the base metals are the lusts and
desire of the flesh. Extracting the
quintessence from these metals, or
transmuting them into higher metals,
is equivalent to setting creative energy
free from the fetters of the sense world.
(metals are symbolic of habits, prejudices
and characteristics)
In each pairing of a planet w/a metal
there is an essential element of the
ambitendent, in that its positive
quality tends one way and its negative
defect tends the other.

        Molten metal is an alchemic symbol
expressing the <u>coniunctio</u> <u>oppositorum</u>
(conjunction of fire and water)

1. Saturn – symbolizes time, with
its ravenous appetite for life,
devours all creations, whether
they be beings, things, ideas or
sentiments. Said to have
devoured his children.

He is related to the Ouroboros – (serpent
which bites its own tail)

Related to the earth, the sarcophagus
and putrefaction as well as the
color black

Mercury – MIND
SUN – Fire of Life
Moon – Memory (water – emotions)
VENUS – manifests all things of the world
          glorified under the radiance
          of the Sun
          – attraction, joy, benefits + gifts
          + cross of matter

~~To the alchemist the Sun~~
~~was the symbol~~

To the alchemists, the
heart was the image of the
sun w/in man just as gold
was the image of the sun
on earth
          – the universal egg – half
silver half gold – Latter
heaven the former earth
Heaven is no. 3 whereas

----

earth is passive (feminine) passive or
material in principle + no. 4
      God wears an Azure veil
over His face – Clouds his
garments, the light of heaven his
ointment which he ~~lubricates~~
anoints his immense body.
Stars – his eyes
Blue – aerial nature
Lead – alchemists employed the image of
the white dove contained in lead to
express their central idea that matter
was the receptical of spirit
Leo (feelings + emotions)

Alembic (carry same sign as intestines

The Star of the Magi
the Morning and Evening Star
Earthly Paradise
Green Tree
the Well
the Dry Tree
Wanderers
Grail
Heathen Grail
Dale
Blessing
The Bride
Waters of Abundance
the Fall
Divine Hand
the Wilderness
Paradise
the Cross shall blossom w/roses
Witch of Atlas

TAROT DIARY

Jod He Vau He   Oct 6, 1964
(4 sacred words)

No VII·
Today cut the chariot (Illusory quest)
14 cords corresponds to No XVI The Tower

Cups are water or water-sprites
red   with passive qualities or
             inertia

good or favorable
conditions
friendly relations

block
Wands or Fire
or elves
active qualities
energy
will
initiative
east

⑦   cords   ⑦   cords

MAN 15 7   9 12   UNIVERSE
                 19
                 18
             17
     6   16
                           west
    0   #21 cord 2.0
          ①   0
I   1   13

  2, 3, 4, 5, 14, 11, 8
         GOD 7

pentacles are earth or gnomes
         14 cords south

Swords
are air
or sylphs

14 cords

14 cords west

evil or
unfavorable
conditions
hostile

14   7
14   7 or 1
14   7
56   21

also the Sphinx
4 merged into one
4 beasts of the
apocalypse

No, 21 includes all the major arcana
it's the circle of time among the 4 elements
or 4 principles (Eagle, (bull) cow, man, lion)
4 letters of the name of God— Yod, He, Vau, & He
4 elements — Fire, water, air & Earth —
              elves, water-sprites, sylphs, & gnomes
              east, south, west & north

The Tower is the results of any artificial rise to power.

No. VII
Today cut <u>The Chariot</u> (Illusory guest)
14 cards corresponds to No XVI The Tower

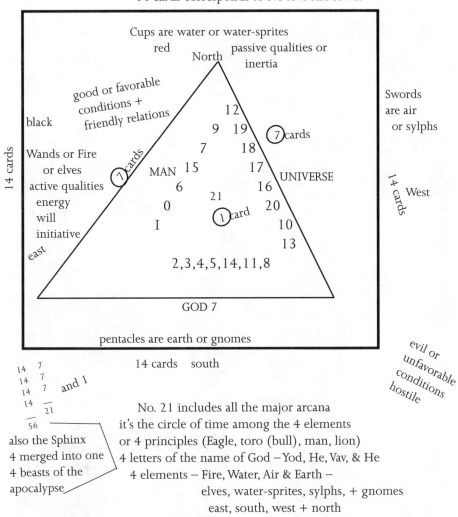

Cups are water or water-sprites
red   passive qualities or
North   inertia

good or favorable
conditions +
friendly relations

Swords
are air
or sylphs

black

Wands or Fire
or elves
active qualities
energy
will
initiative

east

14 cards

7 cards

12
9 19   7 cards
7   18
MAN 15   17
6   16   UNIVERSE
21
0   20
I   1 card   10
13

2,3,4,5,14,11,8

West
14 cards

GOD 7

pentacles are earth or gnomes

14 cards   south

evil or
unfavorable
conditions
hostile

14 7
14 7
14 7 and 1
14 —
    21
  ——
  56

also the Sphinx
4 merged into one
4 beasts of the
apocalypse

No. 21 includes all the major arcana
it's the circle of time among the 4 elements
or 4 principles (Eagle, toro (bull), man, lion)
4 letters of the name of God – Yod, He, Vav, & He
4 elements – Fire, Water, Air & Earth –
elves, water-sprites, sylphs, + gnomes
east, south, west + north

The Tower is the results of any artificial rise to power

Chanting the Square deific — by Whitman!?

~~VII~~ VII Chariot corresponds to XVI
    The Tower

"   "
The Chariot is magic ~~in the~~
sense of incomplete knowledge —
in the sense of "House built
upon sand".   XVI is the fall
which inevitably follows ——
an artificial rise.

         Oct 7, 1964

  this A.M. Cut Death —
    X — XIII Ten Corresponds w/ XIII
Circle is eternity. Serpent is wisdom
The dog "(dog star) (base desire — ". wolf and etc
The Sphinx a monster w/ a lion's body, wings,
and the head & bust of a woman's symbol
of the inscrutable nature of a being.
Everything goes — everything returns.

Black armour; — totally devoid of light etc.
white horse (innocent pure) — rare; fortunate;
auspicious; plume — a token of honor
or prowess — a prize

Chanting the Square deific – by Whitman!?

VII Chariot corresponds to XVI
    The Tower

"The Chariot" is magic in the
sense of incomplete knowledge –
in the sense of "House built
upon sand." XVI is the fall
which inevitably follows
the artificial rise.

Oct 7, 1964

This A.M. Cut Death –
        X – XIII Ten corresponds w/ XIII

Circle is eternity. Serpent is wisdom
the dog "(dog star) . . . (base desire". wolf and etc
[X]   the sphinx – a monster w/ a lion's body, wings,
and the head + bust of a woman; symbol
of the inscrutable nature of a being.
Every thing goes – everything returns

Black armour; – totally devoid of light etc.
[XIII] white horse (innocent, pure) – rare: fortunate;
auspicious – plume – a token of honor
or prowess – a prize

wherever the white steed passed, night & death
followed, flowers withered & leaves fell, the
earth was covered w/a white shroud,
grave-yards appeared — towers, palaces and
cities fell into ruins. — the sun sets in
the background — this is the wheel of
life. — the sun rises on its setting
and sets in its rising — so life dies
when it is born and born when it dies.
Life, Death, sunrise, sunset, are all
thoughts, dreams & fears of the Fool.

Oct. 8. 1964

This A.M. Cut VIII of wands. Up against
a barrier. Stopd dead in my tracks.
Can advance no farther. Wands
are fire & elves — the King, the Ace
the Knight — active qualities — ,
energy, will, initiative, black — ess
the color of wands —
∴ good ie favorable conditions or
friendly relations

wherever the white steed passed, night + death
followed, flowers withered, leaves fell, the
earth was covered w/a white shroud,
grave-yards appeared – towers, palaces and
cities fell into ruins. – the sun sets in
the background. – this is the wheel of
life. – the sun rises in its setting
and sets in its rising – so life dies
when it is born and born when it dies.
Life, Death, sunrise, sunset, are all
thoughts, dreams, + fears of the Fool.

                                        Oct 8, 1964
This A.M. cut VIII of wands. Up against
a barrier. Stopd dead in my tracks.
Can advance no farther. wands
are fire + elves – the king, the Ace,
the seven – active qualities –
energy, will, initiative, black is
the color of wands –
.˙. good, i.e., favorable conditions or
friendly relations

— 15th letter of the alphabet
interchangeably as Zero

eight is used for a rowing or racing team!

Fire: ardor of passion, spirit or, temperament,
liveliness of imagination; Brilliancy, Immensity
hence A STAR; severe trial of affliction
eager. [oxygen, O, 8, 16, 0000 (O = 16)]

          symbol atomic no.   atomic weight

[elements or the traits of a thing]

Elves: mythological being — frail & diminutive
King abbr. "K" (no period) (K as a symbol is the 10th
   Chess: one moves square in any direction
but obliged never to enter or to remain
in check

Ace: one who excels in anything;
Unity, unit, copper coin

[7 — Nitrogen N 14,003 at. wt.]
at. No.   Symbol

Wand 2. a slender flexible rod used,
esp. waved, by one who enchants, con-
jures, or performs feats of legerdemain
; a magician's rod;
— 3. a staff of authority, as a scepter —

15th letter of the alphabet
      interchangeably as zero

    eight is used for rowing or racing team!
Fire: ardor of passion, spirit or, temperament,
     liveliness of imagination; Brilliancy, luminosity
     hence <u>A STAR</u>; severe trial affliction
     eager [oxygen, O, 8, 16,000 (O=16)]

        symbol atomic no. atomic weight

[elements or the traits of a thing]
 Elves: mythological being – frail and diminutive
 King abbr. "K" (no period) ("K" as a symbol is the 10th
     chess: moves one square in any direction
but obliged never to enter or remain
in check
Ace: one who excells in anything;
– unity, unit, copper coin
[7 – Nitrogen N   14.008]
at. no.   symbol   at wt.

<u>Wand</u> 2. a slender flexible <u>rod</u> used,
esp. waved, by one who enhants, con-
jures, or performs feats of legerdemain
; a magician's rod.
– 3. a staff of authority, as a scepter.

Today out X of Pentacles. Pentacles are gnomes.
X is the fourth element & Red is it's suit
color. Pentacles express passive qualities
and inertia. Pentacles signify
evil, i.e., unfavourable or
hostile conditions (relations). Of the
four beasts pentacles represent
the bull. Pentacles element is
earth. The Pentacles are the
fourth letter of God — He.
Pentacles are money or diamonds.
Gnomes — one of the fabled race of
diminutive subterranean beings —
guardians of mines, quarries, etc.
[Possible, Conceivable — mundane]
Pentacles (diamonds) may indicate
worldly & financial success, as well
as distrust and difficulties.
‖ numerical cards — relate to events ‖
Also worldly affairs

*astronomical
⊕
symbol
Earth

also
⊖
or
♁*

Oct 8, 1964

Today cut X of Pentacles. Pentacles are gnomes.
X is the fourth element Fire Red is its suit
color. Pentacles express passive qualities
     and inertia. Pentacles signify
     evil, i.e., unfavorable or
     hostile conditions relations} Of the
     four beasts Pentacles represent
     the bull. Pentacles element is
     earth. The Pentacles are the
     fourth letter of God – He.
     Pentacles are money or diamonds.
     Gnomes – one of the fabled race of
     dimunitive subterranean beings
  – guardians of mines, quarries, etc.
  [Possible, conceivable – mundane]
     Pentacles (diamonds) may indicate
     wordly + financial success, as well as distrust and difficulties.
     Numerical cards – relate to events
     <u>also worldly affaires</u>

X of Pentacles ; money, children success in business ; or marriage ; also a snare. (!)(?)]

inertia : idleness – the property of matter by which it will remain at rest or in uniform motion in the same draught line or direction unless acted upon by some external force. Indisposed to exert or act — inertness

10   neon–ne – atomic wt. 20.183

<u>FIRE</u>   4th Element :

ardor of passion, spirit, or temperament Liveness of imagination —

To animate

inflamed w/ passion

<u>Fourth Principle</u> : result or latent energy

Astrology : the direction – NORTH of the Four Beasts of the Apocalypse : MAN.

Notes for swords or wands on page 161 of "Playing
Cards" book

X of Pentacles: money, children
success in business; or marriage; also
<u>a snare</u> (!) (?)]
inertia: idleness – the property of matter
by which it will remain at rest or in
uniform motion in the same straight
line or direction unless acted upon
by some external force. Indisposed
to exert or act – intertness
10   neon-ne – atomic wt. 20.183
<u>FIRE</u>   4th Element:
        ardor of passion, spirit, or temperament
        Liveness of imagination –
            To animate
                inflamed w/passion
        <u>Fourth Principle</u>: result or latent
            energy
Astrology: the direction – NORTH
    of the Four Beasts of the Apocalypse:
        MAN.

This a.m. Cut XIII of Swords — 3rd letter of Jehovah Vau — this suit expresses equilibrium; "form":

Of the four principles this suit represents Air — of the four classes of spirits this suit represents sylphs; and the direction — West

In the apocalypse it is the beast the eagle.

The XIII is the second principle It is a black suit and express active qualities, energy will & initiative — It is unfavourable conditions or hostile relations.

The card shows a woman bound & blindfolded with 8 swords stuck into the ground behind her and elevation atop which is a city — but she stands upon water.

3 and 5

This A.M. cut XIII of Swords – 3rd letter of
Jehovah <u>Vav</u> – this suit expresses
<u>equilibrium</u>, "<u>form</u>".
   Of the four principles this suit represents
<u>Air</u> – of the four classes of spirits
this suit represents <u>sylphs</u>; and
the direction – <u>West</u>
In the apocalypse it is the beast
the <u>eagles</u>.
   The XIII is the second principle
It is a black suit and expresses active
qualities, energy will initiative –
It is <u>unfavorable</u> <u>conditions</u>
or <u>hostile</u> <u>relations</u>.

The card shows a woman bound + blindfolded
with 8 swords stuck into the ground.
Behind her an elevation atop which
is a city – but she stands upon water.

   3 and 5

The compass has 32 points of direction
and the 360 degrees of the circle.

she has five swords to her left
and two to her right — one
to the right of her is slightly
to front. It is a dismal picture
of a captive.

Sword: Something that kills, destroys,
punishes etc. 3. a symbol of power;
as: a. Judicial or legal authority 4.
military power,

Chemical element: oxygen O 8
at. wt 16,0000

The form is the pattern or schema. 2.
a manner or method of expression — formal
way of proceeding

Sylphe: imaginary being inhabiting the air
a noune given by Paracelsus to the
elemental beings of the air.
Conceived as mortal by soulless.
(a slender graceful woman)

to the left: weaker side also insincere
malicious,

[the compass has 32 points of direction
        and the 360 degrees of the circle.]

she has five swords to her left
and two to her right – one
to the right of her is slightly
to front. It is a dismal picture
of a captive.
    Sword: something that kills, destroys,
    punishes etc. 3. A symbol of power;
    as: a. Judicial or legal authority 4.
    military power.
Chemical element: oxygen   O   8
            at wt 16 0000
The form is the pattern or schema 2.
a manner or method of expression – formal
way of proceeding

Sylph: imaginary being inhabiting the air
  a name given by Paracelsus to the
  elemental beings of the air.
  Conceived as mortal by soulless.
  (a slender graceful woman)
to the left: weaker side also insincere
malicious.

Spades 9 or (swords) seem to be regarded as the worst suit. The XIII of swords (clubs) denote treachery, disappointment, death and other unpleasantness — it is regarded as the worst (unluckiest) card in the pack. — sd to have been a superstition of Napoleon.

Court cards relate to people while numerical cards relate to events. Spades (swords) relate to 'the serious affairs of life'.

XIII of swords: Help & danger loss. (a card of warning)!!??
EVENTS?

spades or (swords) seem to be regarded as
the worst suit. The XIII of swords
(clubs) denote treachery, disappointment,
death and other unpleasantness – it is
regarded as the worst (unluckiest) card in the
pack. – sd to have been a superstition   of
Napoleon.

Court cards relate to people
while numerical cards relate to events
Spades (swords) relate to the <u>serious</u>
 <u>affaires of life</u>

XIII of swords: Help, danger, loss.
              (a card of warning)!!??
                        EVENTS?

Today cut Queen of Cups. Cups are water
or waterspirits & Queen stands for water.
A red suit. Cups express passive qualities
and inertia. Cup signify good, that is,
favourable conditions.

Cup represent {
Alchemy: water
Astrology: South
Apocalypse: head of a lion

Cup or Cups can be construed as
referring to the affections
– a fair or brown-haired woman;
faithful and affectionate

Cup: that which is to be received, whether
to enjoy or endure; a potion.

Astronomy: Aquarius
~~Water~~ the 11th sign of the Zodiac
" ♒ "

Oct 9, 1964

Today cut Queen of Cups. Cups are water
or water spirits. Queen stands for water.
A red suit. Cups express passive qualities
and inertia. Cup signify good, that is,
favourable conditions.

	Alchemy: water
Cup represent	Astrology: South
	Apocalypse: head of a lion

Cup or Hearts can be construed as
referring to affections
– A fair or brown-haired woman;
faithful and affectionate
Cup: that which is to be rescued, whether
to enjoy or endure; a portion.
Astronomy: Aquarius
            the 11th sign of the Zodiac

Aries, Ram ♈   Scorpio, Scorpio ♏
Taurus, Bull ♉   nov 21 Sagittarius, Archer, ♐
Gemini, Twins ♊   Dec 21 Capricornus, Goat ♑
Cancer, Crab ♋   Aquarius, Water Bearer, ♒
Leo, Lion, ♌   Pisces, Fishes, ♓
Virgo, Virgin ♍
Libra, Balance, ♎

                                        Oct 10, 1964

Today cut the X of Pentacles. It is the
last letter of the Name of God — "He"
the ~~fourt~~ fourth, result or latent
energy. The Pentacles relate to
events. Its direction is North
in ~~Astrology~~; In magic it earth
of gnomes. Of the apocalypse it
is the fourth w/ the head of a MAN.
The color is red and expresses positive
Qualities and inertia. They ~~express~~
signify soil i.e. unfavorable
constellations   or hostile relations

Aries, Ram	Scorpio, Scorpio
Taurus, Bull	Nov 21 Sagittarius, Archer
Gemini, Twins	Dec 21 Capricornus, Goat
Cancer, Crab	Aquarius, Water Bearer
Leo, Lion	Pisces, Fishes
Virgo, Virgin	
Libra, Balance	

Oct 10, 1964

Today cut the V of Pentacles. It is the
last letter of the Name of God – "He"
the fourth result of latent
energy. The V Pentacles relate to
events. Its direction is North.
In ~~Astrology~~ : In magic it earth
of gnomes. Of the Apocalypse it
is the fourth w/the head of MAN.
The color is red and expresses passive
qualities and inertia. They ~~express~~
signify evil i.e. unfavorable
conditions or hostile relations

we americans with our "nigger" heritage
what else are we but the casta-offs
of Europe; And that's not all nor is
it the end of it. We will come
upon no better days than now.
Being is a state of permanence —
the clock being aside — the "now"
that's the moment of action
                                    Oct 11, 1964

Today (A.M. Cut The High Priestess) II
this card corresponds w/ card no. XXI
The World. Card no II is said to be
Fae, or hidden knowledge. Its opposite
card, The World XXI is said to be
in the circle of Time in the midst of the
four principles, that is, the object of
knowledge. (also they are the four beasts
beings of the Apocalypse,
Card II   The Two columns   B J
the left Block and the right light.
So Tiara of the 2 horned moon.
Veil behind w/ green leaves   and

we americans with our "nigger" heritage
what else are we but the casts-offs
of Europe; and that's not all nor is
it the end of it. We will come
upon no better days than now.
Being is a state of permanence –
the clock being aside – the "now"
that's the moment of action

                        Oct 11, 1964

Today (A.M. cut the High Priestess) II
this card corrresponds w/card no. XXI
The World. Card no II is said to be
Isis, or hidden <u>knowledge</u>. II's opposite
card, the World XXI is said to be
in the circle of Time in the midst of the
four principles, that is, the object of
<u>knowledge</u>. (also they are the four
beings of the Apocalypse.
Card II <u>The Two Columns</u> BJ
the left Black and the right light.
Tiara of the 2 horned moon.
Veil behind w/green leaves and

see if book on Knight Templars

red pomegranate fruits.
The image of the World must
be understood before one can
pass into the Gates of the Temple.

Isis (Egyptian Godess of motherhood
and fertility sometimes represented
as Cowhended. She is sister and
wife of Osiris,

(Roman Ceres) Demeter — Godess of the fruitful soil,
of agriculture and of the fruitfulness
of mankind and guardian of
marriage — Her daughter Prosepina
or Persepine married Pluto or (Hades)

Oct 15

Today Cut King of Swords —
Swords represent Hatred & Misfortune
King represent a man
— active — Positive Swords
represent Dark people
He is a dark — bad man. He
is a soldier, a powerful enemy
who must be distrusted.

see if book on Knight Templars

red pomegranate fruits.
The image of the World must
be understood before one can
pass into the Gates of the Temple.

Isis   (Egyptian goddess of motherhood
and Fertility sometimes represented
as cowheaded. She is sister and
wife of Osiris.

(Roman Ceres) Demeter – Goddess of the fruitful soil,
of agriculture and of the fruitfulness
of mankind and guardian of
marrriage – Her daughter Proserpina
or Persepine married Pluto or (Hades)

Oct 15

Today cut King of Swords –
Swords represent Hatred + Misfortune
King represent a man
– active – Positive Swords
represent Dark people
He is a dark – bad – man, He
is a soldier, a powerful enemy
who must be distrusted.

~~Names given King of Clubs~~
~~Alexander, Clovis, Julius Caesar,~~
~~Arthur (Arthur), Hector, Annibal~~
~~Bl. ...~~

Name given Swords (spades)
(David!) ~~...~~ apollin (
constantine, ninus, Scipio, Godfrey
de Bouillon — cupid's useless darts

Swords (spades) denote treachery,
disapointment, death and other
unpleasantnesses.
Court Cards ~~are~~ indicate people.

King g Swords: A very dark man,
unscrupulous and ambitious
(also a widower)
Vau - the third letter of God = equilibrium
Alchemy: Air. & ~~sulphur~~
magic: sylphs
Astrology: West
Apocalypse: head of an eagle

Names given king of Clubs
Alexander, Clovis, Julius Caesar,
Artus (Arthur), Hector, Annibal –
Sir Oliver Rant

Names given Swords (spades)
(David (!)) Apollin
Constantine, Ninus, Scipio, Godfrey
de Bouillon – cupid's useless darts

Swords (spades) denote treachery,
disappointment, death and other
unpleasantness.
Court cards indicate people.

King of Swords: A very dark man;
unscrupulous and ambitious
(also a widower)
Vav – the third letter of God = equilibrium
Alchemy: Air + sylphs
Magic: sylphs
Astrology: West
Apocalypse: head of an eagle

It is a black suit.

Oct 15, 1964

Cut Card No. 0.
    0. corresponds to I, The
Magician.
    The Fool ~~is critical man~~,
is individual man, a weak
man. Together w/ Card No. I
The Juggler, depicts Superman,
or mankind as a whole,
Connecting earth and heaven.
No I is Adam Kadmon (humanity or Superman)
    It is the First seven of the triangle.

man   God
    10, IV, 15, 99, 12

        Universe

It is a black suit.

Oct 15, 1964
Cut card no. 0
0 corresponds to I, The
Magician
The Fool is artificial man,
is individual man, a weak
man. Together w/card No. I
The Juggler, depicts Superman,
or mankind as a whole,
connecting earth and heaven.
No I is Adam Kadmon (humanity or Superman)
It is the First Seven of the triangle:

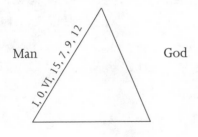

Man   God

Universe

over his head is the sign of the eternity ∞. the wand he holds is the sign of Fire, the pentacle is the sign of earth — the cup & sword is the sign of water & Air.

Oct 16, 1964

cut No. VII The Chariot — is magic in the sense of incomplete knowledge — in the sense of "the house built upon sand" and it's opposite card no. XVI The Tower — is the fall which inevitably follows an artificial rise. The Chariot, in other words is the "illusory quest"—

The first seven I, O, VI, XV, VII, IX, XII, refer to Man — i.e;

The pictures must be taken according to their meaning — not according to their order. Here (in this pair of cards — VII & XVI; VII is in the order of Man i.e one of the seven steps in the path of man. 1s the changes in

over his head is the sign of
the eternity ∞. The wand he holds
is the sign of Fire, the pentacle is
the sign of earth – the cup + sword is
the sign of water + air

Oct 16, 1964

Cut No. VII The Chariot – is magic in
the sense of incomplete knowledge – in
the sense of "the house built upon sand"
and it's opposite card no. XVI
The Tower – is the fall which
inevitably follows an artificial rise.
The Chariot, in other words is the
"illusory guest" –

The first seven I, 0, VI, XV, VII, IX, XII,
refer to Man – i.e.

The pictures must be taken according to
their meaning – not according to their
order. Here (in this pair of cards –
VII + XVI; VII is in the order of
Man i.e. one of the seven steps in the
path of man. i.e. the changes in

personality of a man. However it's
correspondent No XVI in in
the second seven – The Universe –
is, the second seven in some
way connect man with God in
the universe. There is a great
truth to be obtained from these
two corresponding cards.

business at hand to
discern among sheep
  the goats there
hot holed the canvas
  beneath that
all men equally
out g reach
under wings then as all
incarnation a song
  peter & out
I carried into a sea un-
  noticed et mon décor
laurel yr. pet de loups in –
consequent as the rest

mediocrity's the
elevator Sign's
  ass inde up
writing ass
  wipe's paper
ta ta bleys
  well
moeurs contempor-
ine that a
jock-strap
hung
loprudently
a bulge

personality of a man. However its
correspondent No. XVI is in
the second seven – The Universe
i.e. the second seven in some
way connect man with God in
the Universe. There is a great
truth to be obtained from these
two corresponding cards.

---

business at hand to
discern among sheep
    the goats there
hot holed the canvas
    beneath that
all men equally
 out of reach
under wings then as all
incarnation a song
    peterd out
Icarus'd into a sea un-
    noticed et non décor
laurel yr pet de loups in-
    consequent as the rest

mediocrity's the
elevator sign's
ass side up
writing as
wipe paper
ta ta sleep
    well
moeurs contempor
raire shit a
jock-strap
  hung
lopsidedly
  a bulge

Oct 16, 1964

Today cut IV of Wands : Wands
are Fire and in Astrology the direction
East, of the apocalypse it is the
Bull, and it is in color — block
suit — and by press active qualities.
it is a Good suit, expresses favorable
conditions or friendly relations.
∴ 4 of Clubs (wands) : Changes
inconstancy (a Cord of warning)

The MAGICIAN : The original activity
and the creative power of man
∞ infinity over his head :
wand in his right hand, clubs,
cups, pentacle on the Table,
all correspond to the 4 Elements.
Master over a given situation,
red jacket — Activity — the
enigma is related to Mercury

236

October 16, 1964

Today cut IV of Wands: Wands
are Fire and in Astrology the direction
East, of the Apocalypse it is the
Bull and it is in color – black
suit – and express active qualities.
It is a <u>Good</u> suit – expresses favorable
conditions or friendly relations.
  · 4 of Clubs (Wands): changes
<u>inconstancy (a card of warning)</u>

The MAGICIAN: The original activity
and the creative power of Man
∞ infinity over his head.
<u>Wand</u> in his right hand, clubs,
cups, pentacles on the table.
All correspond to the 4 Elements
Master over a given situation.
red jacket – <u>Activity</u> – the
enigma is related to <u>Mercury</u>

Notes: In Greek legends, lameness usually symbolizes some defect of the Spirit — some essential blemish.

Oct 17, 1964

Today cut No. XV The Devil. This card corresponds w/card No. XI Justice. Card No. XI. Justice is Truth. No XV The Devil is lie.

The Devil is Baphomet (of the Knights Templars) He has head & feet of a he-goat and the bosom & arms of a woman. It incorporates the four elements: black legs: Earth & the Spirits of the nether world; the scales on its flanks to water dissolution; its blue wings to sylphs— its red head to fire.

Disorder & perversion - desire Stagnation all its passionate

Notes: In Greek legends, lameness
usually symbolizes some defect
of the Spirit – some essential
blemish.

Oct 17, 1964

Today cut No. XV The Devil.
This card corresponds w/card
No. XI Justice. Card No. XI
<u>Justice</u> is Truth. No XV the Devil is
<u>lie</u>.
    The Devil is Baphomet (of the
Knights Templars) He has head
+ feet of a he-goat and the
bosom + arms of a woman.
It incorporates the four elements:
black legs: Earth + the spirits of
the nether world; the scales
on its flanks to <u>water</u> dissolution;
its blue wings to sylphs – its red
head to <u>fire</u>.
Disorder + pervesion – desire
stagnation all its passionate

form,

<u>Justice</u> XI : exact, bilateral
equilibrium — Scales are symbolic of
equilibrium, of good & evil. —
Also The Word of God — The enigma
is related to libra, Justice
is astrea, The Devil is the
product of human lies. Men
invented the Devil in order to
have justification for themselves —
to regard him as the cause
of wrongdoing.   Oct 18, 1964
Cut The Sun No XIX.   No XIX
Corresponds w/ card   No IV The
Emperor.   The great Laws Four.
The alpha & omega of it all.
Action — Four signs of the Tarot
Resistance, completion, results.
The Sun is the Expression of the
Fiery Word & The sign of the Emperor.

form.

Justice XI: exact, bilateral
equilibrium – Scales are symbolic of
equilibrium; of good and evil.
Also The Word of God – The enigma
is related to libra. Justice
is astrea. The Devil is the
product of human lies. Men
invented the Devil in order to
have justification for themselves –
to regard him as the cause
of wrongdoing.
                           Oct 18, 1964
Cut the Sun No XIX   No XIX
corresponds to w/card No IV The
Emperor.   The great Law of Four.
The Alpha + Omega of it all.
Action – Four signs of the Tarot
Resistance, Completion, results.
The Sun is the Expression of the
Fiery Word + the sign of The Emperor.

Oct 20, 1964

The Judgement – No XX Corresponds
with No III the Empress. The latter
is Nature in all its aspects.
No XX is also Nature in all its eternally
reviviging + regenerating activity.
No. XX is in the second side
of the triangle i.e, Universe while
it's corresponding card No III is in
the God or third side of the
Triangle.

Oct 22, 1964

Today cut Card No XVII the
Star and it corresponds w/card
No. VI the Lovers.
No. VI is Temptation or Lovers
— the emotional side of life while
its corresponding card No XVII
The Star or (The Astral World)
is the emotional side of Nature.
They have ceased to listen to
the guiding voice of Poetry
they seek to dominate by

Oct 20, 1964

The Judgement – No XX Corresponds
with No III The Empress. The latter
is Nature in all its aspects.
No XX is also Nature in all its eternally
revivifying – regenerating activity.
No. XX is in the second side
of the triangle i.e. <u>Universe</u> while
its corresponding card No III is in
the <u>God</u> or third side of the
triangle.

Oct 22, 1964

Today cut card No. XVII The
Star and it corresponds w/card
No. VI the Lovers.
– the emotional side of life while
its corresponding card No XVII
The Star or (The Astral World)
is the emotional side of Nature.
<u>They have ceased to listen</u> to
the guiding voice of Poetry
they seek to dominate by

ingenuity & intellection.   2 tokes
                              eat cigarettes
The world of the imagination is for ever
closed to them — only by great
suffering can man pass out of
the power of death & return to life.

The Stor No. XVII the imagination of
Nature — She dreams, imagines, creates
worlds. Learn to write your imagination
w/ that of hero & nothing is impossible.
He Is a choise.

_____

flee over street humping
Roy wise the blocked out   but what if others
   faces door bolt down rhodes   what others they
cornered "paranoia" write that   're dead sign
down peck I do it's Hell   in the book
                                 Faustus sold
   when halfway thru Faustus   out before
wine pills muffled bell keep   but you're in
   the out the dead already out Hell already
                                 sign in
write signs in the book Faustus commands me do it   the book.

ingenuity of intellection.
The world of the imagination is forever
closed to them – <u>Only by great</u>
<u>suffering</u> can man pass out of
the power of death + return to life.

The Star No. XVII the imagination of
Nature – She dreams, imagines, creates
worlds. Learn to unite your imagination
w/that of hers + nothing is impossible.
<u>He is a choice.</u>

flee over street humping
dog wise blacked out
    faces door bolt drawn shades
cornered "paranoia" write that
down Jack I do it's Hell
    half-way thru Faustus
wine fills muffled bell keep
   the dead already out
write signs in the book Faustus commands me to do it

but what of others
what others they
are dead sign
in the book
Faustus sold
out before,
but you're in
Hell already
sign in
the book.

The Ten Sephiroth from what power, glory, vitalitis attribute principles were unfolded or pro- duced —

I. Kether, the Supreme Crown.
II. Chokmah, wisdom
III. Binah, intelligence or understanding.
IV. Chesed, mercy otherwise = Gedulah, magnificence
V. Geburah, severity, judgement, awe, power
VI. Tiphareth, Beauty.
VII. Netzach, Victory
VIII. Hod, Glory
IX. Yesod, the foundation
X. Malkuth, the Kingdom

?

I The Juggler —
II The Priestess —
III The Empress —
IIII The Emperor
XI The Wheel
XX Day of Judgment
XIX ~ XVIII The Sun

IV The Emperor

V The Hierophant ~ XVIII The Moon Cards

VI Temptation   XVII The Star
VII The Chariot   XVI The Tower
VIII Justice   XV The Devil
IX The Hermit   XIV Temperance
X The Wheel of Fortune XIII Death

XI Strength   XII The Hanged Man

The ten Sephiroth from which powers, forces, vitalities, attributes principles were unfolded or produced –

I Kether, the Supreme Crown
II Chokmah, wisdom
III Binah, intelligence or understanding
IV Chesed, mercy otherwise Gedulah, magnificence or Benignity and Greatness
V Geburah, Severity, Judgement [?], Power
VI Triphereth, Beauty
VII Netzach, Victory
VIII Hod, Glory
IX Yesod, the Foundation
X Malkuth, The Kingdom
?

I The Juggler   XXI the world
II Priestess   XX Day of Judgment
III Empress
IV The Emperor   XIX The Sun
V The Hierophant or XVIII The Moon (also referred to "Astrology")
VI Temptation   XVII The Star
VII The Chariot   XVI The Tower
VIII Justice   XV The Devil
IX The Hermit   XIV Temperance
X The Wheel of Fortune XIII Death
XI Strength   XII "The Hanged Man"

Postscript

> "it's easier to explain whereto and fores of alchemy than tackle the
> Jonas mystery"
>
> —Stephen Jonas, from a 1968 notebook

When Stephen Jonas died on February 10, 1970, he consigned the secret of his origins to the grave. The palimpsest of pseudo-biographical and anti-biographical stories he left behind in his notebooks and letters seem to have been penned for multiple reasons: for his own amusement, especially when written to confound or subvert the expectations and curiosity of his white acquaintances; as the expression of his latent, dynamic talent for writing fiction; and when deposited in private notebooks no one else would be paging through, the compulsive backfilling of what might have been a genuine void of self-knowledge, an authentic amnesia. His anti-biographical narratives were performances in which he appeared to yield to the inquisitiveness of his associates when in fact he was reasserting his own agency to define and re-define himself, to maintain mystery and reassert his right to withhold crucial details, or fabricate spurious ones. So it is with some ambivalence I went digging into Stephen Jonas's past, not to pigeonhole Jonas or lay bare his posthumous secrets but to explore the depth and richness of his tales and to provide context from the Massachusetts he hardly ever left.

Most of his stories are dependent on a single repeating theme, a Catholic upbringing located on the South Coast of Massachusetts from which he was severed, either by adoption by whites or by his own search for Protestant acceptance. Jonas claimed to have been born to parents from Cabo Verde, islands off the west coast of Africa which, during Jonas's lifetime, were either a colony or province of Portugal, and now form an independent republic. New Bedford, Massachusetts, due to its whaling industry attracting migrant workers, became the prime city of the Cabo Verdean diaspora in the United States. Other versions give Jonas a Spanish-speaking origin and middle-class Puerto Rican forebears on his mother's side, and a relocation from Massachusetts to Plainfield, New Jersey. In each re-telling Jonas brought fresh modifications. Several who were closest to Jonas came to accept the basic premise he had been born Rufus Jones in Georgia and that, at some point in his youth, he had migrated north. His accent, however, was staunchly Massachusetts without a Southern trace, as anyone can now hear thanks to the website for Harvard's Woodberry Poetry Room.[1] To my ears—and I've never lived outside Massachusetts—Jonas's accent sounds unfeigned, the voice of a bookish son of the lower middle class, and I can't imagine Jonas spent much formative time outside the Bay State.

We also have his listing on the Social Security Death Index giving his legal name as Stephen Jonas (rather than Rufus Jones), his birthdate as December 1, 1921, his February 1970 death in Boston—but the number's state of issuance as Georgia. Since the first Social Security cards were assigned in 1936 Jonas was no younger than fifteen when he received his, keeping open the possibility the name Jonas was an alias taken on early. It may have been military service instead of birth that placed Jonas in Georgia. He often received treatment at the VA mental health facility in Brockton, Massachusetts. He was in Georgia for some time, long enough to receive his card, but that's all we know for now.

Between the fact of a Georgia-issued Social Security number and a voice speaking in a credible native Massachusetts accent we have threads of Jonas's stories spun during his last twenty years of life—spun and tangled together. I noticed a curious line demarcating his narratives: 1948. His writing pops with particular city landmarks, verifiable people, plausible incidents when describing 1948 and after. Before that, the Depression years, improbable tales written with gusto and humor. And in between, the World War II years, is a lacuna, a span of silence; whether any of his ensuing mental health challenges arose due to war experiences is entirely a matter of speculation.

Names changed: Stephen R. Jonas. Rufus S. Jones. Peter Santos. Luiz Santos. In one 1968 notebook entry, Stephen Jonas Manual Edwards Perreira y Santos. If Jonas was his name from birth, and if his accent did indeed signal a Bay State childhood, two options leap out. A Jonas family is enrolled in the Mashpee Wampanoag Indian Tribal Council, a Native American tribe located in Mashpee, Massachusetts on the southwestern shoulder of Cape Cod.[2] In census records Jonases in Mashpee, like many Mashpee Wampanoag, have been categorized alternatively as "Indian" or "Black" due to marriages with African American mariners early in the nineteenth century. Although Jonas did not claim to be Mashpee Wampanoag to friends, in one 1968 notebook he related a conversation from 1955: "Cynthia said your people American Indians? told her fergit baby it's a bad scene anyway." I can't connect Stephen Jonas to the Jonas family of Mashpee, Massachusetts but considering the coincidence of names and the notebook entry, it's worth putting the possibility down on paper.

The other major option is Cabo Verdean. Jonas frequently claimed to be the son of a Cabo Verdean father, although not one named Jonas; however, there were Jonas families from Cabo Verde, and first-generation Americans of Cabo Verdean descent, living in New Bedford, Marion, Carver, Grafton, Boston, Mattapoisett, Hanson, and other municipalities in Massachusetts during the time of Stephen Jonas's childhood, often working in cranberry bogs or textile mills. Again and again Jonas placed his origin in New Bedford, although the narratives frequently dwelled on severance from his Cabo Verdea birth parents, Cabo Verdean culture, the Portuguese language, and the adoption of a Protestant identity, even of a WASP partisanship on behalf of what Jonas called "Henry James' America." He once wrote in a 1966 notebook, regarding Quakers who perhaps adopted him: "I owe all to the Friends. Genuine & forthright, tho they have their prejudices." The New Bedford Children's Aid Society, a "placing out" organization, formerly the New Bedford Orphan's Home, was operating during the years of Jonas's childhood. It's possible he was in the Society's custody as a child and placed with a private (Quaker) family. "[I] don't by any means claim an affinity to this heritage taken off the streets, at most, an adoption." He wrote, "The graft took." And, later, "Left on streets of New Bedford, God knows where I wld have ended up."

Many times he claimed Santos as his original surname. Recounting a 1959 arrest in a notebook, Jonas puts this question in the investigating officer's mouth: "but then you were Peter Santos?" Jonas wrote the response: "Pleaded amnesia and the book of Job." Santos arises again in a 1956 letter to aspiring poet and protégé Edward Marshall, although in this case the Santos name is tied to a Spanish-speaking rather than Cabo Verdean origin. The name Rufus S. Jones, he told Marshall, was assumed in adulthood in honor of the well-regarded Quaker theologian who, at that time, enjoyed a glowing national reputation. In another notebook entry he described himself as being the son of a New Bedford fisherman named Manuel or Peter Santos, Jonas being, according to his note, "one of seven born w/ none entered on birth records which could (if I cared to) explain a great mystery to the Government Federal who pay for their bungling (monthly)." The 1930 census does show a Cabo Verdean laborer named Peter Santos in New Bedford, the father of seven children, although it is not clear which of those children could be Stephen Jonas.[3] However, the story of Peter Santos and his seven children is prefaced by a tall tale regarding an ancestor named "Peter Grady Edwards" from South Carolina who married a "Brown's Circus performer later P.T. Barnum—birth defect of web legs but separated by operation (Boston 1889)," but "no word in New Bedford of the Perreira freak no recurrances to date." It is supposedly a daughter of this mermaid circus performer who "married father Manuel (Peter) Santos free thinking lobster fisherman." Ending this section, Jonas wrote: "anyway I'm crazy so Dr. Lovel keeps passing out the pills (how are you this month?) but his progenitor did not sign the Articles of Ratification commenced the Republic, so it's easier to explain the whereto and fores of alchemy than tackle the Jonas mystery. [A]merican but easier to deny nativity than explain bewildered second generation or 3rd."

Most elaborate by far of the anti-biographical texts is "What Made Maud Hum," set in Plainfield, New Jersey among a community of Christian Scientists. It seems Jonas worked at the Christian Science Complex in Boston in the late

1940s;[4] whether he got the job through Christian Scientist connections in New Jersey or knew the landscape of Christian Science from his Boston work in unclear. In "Maud" Jonas placed his origin among middle-class Puerto Rican emigrees in St. Augustine, Florida and New Jersey on his mother's side, New Bedford fishermen, perhaps Cabo Verdean, on his father's. Although a German-American family named Jonas did live in the Plainfield area,[5] the characters of Maud cannot be correlated with confidence to any family in censuses or city directories, with the exception, perhaps, of the Glickmans, who might possibly be a husband and wife chiropractic team of the same name working in Plainfield during the "Maud" time-frame.[6] Another possibly real figure was the George Dayhof who Jonas said drove to York, Pennsylvania from Philadelphia with him, weeping over the death of President Franklin Roosevelt. A George Dayhof or Dehoff was living in York at that time. A coincidence? Perhaps.

Despite the repeating element of a lost Catholic Puerto Rican or Cabo Verdean heritage, "Maud" is unique among the anti-biographical writings for staging Jonas's childhood not only outside Massachusetts but in a city that was a major destination for African Americans during the Great Migration. About half of Plainfield's population today is African American. And it is not the first time Jonas tied himself to Christian Science: to Edward Marshall he claimed to have joined a Christian Science youth organization while enrolled at Boston University. Reading "Maud" closely, however, makes clear the glaring lack of place names, of local specifics; streets, stores, hotels, parks, schools are anonymous, although the story abounds with personal names. According to the Social Security Death Index Jonas would've been about twelve when Franklin Roosevelt—frequent topic of heated conversations in "Maud"— took office yet the urban landscape is hard to grasp. So too, for that matter, is New Bedford. Again, 1948 has the feel of a new beginning, a concrete environment, but what is described as taking place before is a bright, tight focus on immediate family ringed by shadows; the outer world filters in through elders' talk.

When authorities came for Stephen Jonas's body a close friend gave his name as Rufus S. Jones, meaning his death certificate bears that name; the Boston city registrar and the Social Security file agree on two things: the significance of Georgia, and a 1921 birth. African American men named Rufus Jones of the approximate right age I've located on Georgia censuses have been otherwise accounted for. In 1966, however, Jonas did write in a notebook, "And as for Rufus Jones (George Wurnn's query) dead, I think this eleven years and they can't prove it." That Georgia may have been the site of Jonas's military service is complicated by the lack of a match for Jonas either on draft registration cards or in the Veterans Affairs benificiary identification records, although notes for appointments at the Brockton VA can be found in his notebooks.

According to longtime friend Raffael De Gruttola, Jonas worked at the South Boston Army Base in 1950 as a civilian bureaucrat when he met Raffael's brother Dante, becoming afterwards a frequent visitor to the De Gruttola home in Somerville. Jonas didn't mention the South Boston Army Base in his anti-biographical writings. Perhaps little or nothing of his lived reality came to be used as raw material for his tales.

However, a poem called "XXXIII" is an extended account of Jonas's time in post-World War II Boston, and the personages and places came up verifiable. "Menden" Sewell was Minden Sewell, an English-born singer and former wife of an American violinist; she later worked as a publicist for the Boston Tuberculosis Association. Emily Huntington may have been a Simmons College economics instructor of the same name. Sewell lived at 10 Clearway St., Boston, which is adjacent to the Mary Baker Eddy Library of the Christian Science headquarters.[7] "The Napoleon" was the Napoleon Club, a gay bar in the Bay Village neighborhood of Boston. Boston University was, as Jonas wrote, then a commuter school located in Copley Square before its 1950s move to Charles River's western banks.

Prior to the arrival of aspiring poets Jack Spicer and Robin Blaser from San Francisco, Jonas may have studied composition with Cid Corman, known for his poetry radio broadcasts on WMEX, and his magazine, Origin. Already in 1953 he could produce a formidable list of Elizabethan and Modernist poets for Edward Marshall to read. Jonas must've been a voracious reader and skilled autodidact. Prescott Townsend, who also appears in "XXXIII," the patrician-born advocate for gay rights in Boston, whose portfolio of rental properties primarily on the "back side" of Beacon Hill near Scollay Square sustained Boston's Bohemian and Queer scene for multiple decades, is extensively discussed by Douglass Shand-Tucci in his study The Crimson Letter.[8] The heyday of Townsend's performance space the Barn at 36 Joy Street, a brick building which was a former carriage house, was long gone by the time Jonas came into Townsend's orbit, but in former years the Barn had hosted a succession of short-lived dramatic groups, including The Boston Stage Society, The Experimental Theatre, The Ford Hall Forum Dramatic Society, The Boston Players, and the New England Repertory Players, producing works such as the Soviet writer Valentin Kataev's Squaring the Circle (1928) and the Austrian playwright Arthur Schnitzler's Anatol (1893). In Jonas's time, by all accounts, the Townsend scene had lost its artistic character, becoming more of a refuge for the addicted, exhausted, and persecuted.[9]

Another figure from Boston's upper crust Jonas mentions in "XXXIII" is Avery Peabody, son of a leather merchant, during the time of his association with Jonas working a bookstall, perhaps allowing Jonas to crash with him. An Avery S. Peabody, son of a Newton leather manufacturer, did briefly run a bookstore in Boston out of his 124 Mt. Vernon St. home in the year 1948,[10] but seemingly not before or after. So Jonas decided to give us solid ground when he stated in the poem "wuz abt '48 or '9 on Mt. Vernon St. . . ."

Stephen Jonas's first appearance in the Boston City Directory is in 1954: he is listed as "Steph. R. Jonas, student" living at 316 Huntington Avenue, address of a largescale YMCA. If he was born in 1921 he would've been approximately 33, yet still taking night classes or part-time courses without employment; how he paid for them beyond perhaps the G.I. Bill is uknown. Next time is 1958, and he called himself a writer, as well as editor for *Measure* magazine (John Wieners' three-issue little magazine), living at 14 Irving St. He was, then, squarely on the "back" of Beacon Hill in the orbit of Prescott Townsend. A later move to Garden Street kept him in Townsend's orbit, but his relocation to Saint Charles Street in the mid-1960s set him in the South End up against I-90. His 1970 death occurred at 24 Anderson St., a return to Beacon Hill. In each case the Directory gives his occupation as "writer" or lacks an occupation, so there was no further income besides what must've been a disability check.

In 1953, on Boston Common Jonas had a chance encounter with Edward Marshall, an aspiring white poet, then twenty-one, who had been born in New Hampshire with family roots in Gloucester, Massachusetts (locus of Charles Olson's *Maximus Poems*). In addition to Jonas's confidently dispensed syllabus of Early Modern and Modernist poets, he attempted to sway Marshall away from his Christian vocation, from Protestantism—Episcopalianism, specifically—Jonas having repudiated his own Protestant turn. In his relationship with Marshall, Jonas was mentor, clearly in the dominant role. After Marshall left Boston for New York he published his tour de force poem "Leave the Word Alone" in the *Black Mountain Review*, organ of experimental Black Mountain College in North Carolina; the poem was a sensation on campus, widely discussed and praised, later anthologized by Donald Allen in his *The New American Poetry* (1960). In the poem, which is a ten-page confession of inherited mental illness and genealogical puzzles reminiscent of Jonas's own anti-biographical work, a poem that does not so much conclude as majestically expend its steam, Marshall mentions himself surviving "under Steve," an ability he ascribed to his Nova Scotian blood allowing him to "get butch." Left in Boston, beyond the burgeoning New York scene, Jonas penned "To a Strayed Cat," his riposte to Marshall: "5 months you were destitute," it begins, "Destitute / and w/o that traffic of loves / who now pursue U / I took you in."

At the Charles Street Meeting House, on the "flat," rather than the "back," of Beacon Hill, Jonas heard Charles Olson, the rector of Black Mountain College, give a major reading in the Autumn of 1954, either in September on a date later supplied by John Wieners, or in October, when Hurricane Hazel made

Massachusetts landfall. Due to this experience Wieners made contact with Black Mountain College, and enrolled. One of Wieners' friends from Boston College, Joe Dunn, who went on to operate White Rabbit Press, was also in attendance, following Wieners to North Carolina, but moving on shortly thereafter. Boston, however, had activity of its own, and Jonas, by staying in town, was able to form the nucleus of a new poets' group with "Berkeley Renaissance" figures Jack Spicer and Robin Blaser, both having found work as librarians, Spicer at the Boston Public Library, Blaser at Harvard. Lewis Ellingham and Kevin Killian in their biography of Jack Spicer, *Poet Be Like God* cover this period, and these poets, extensively.[11] This "Occult School of Boston," as it was christened later, produced a single anthology called *The Boston Newsletter* (n.d., 1956), with poems by Blaser, Spicer, Dunn, Wieners, and Jonas; they also staged a reading on September 23, 1956 at 38 Grove St.

Even though Spicer and Blaser split Boston, returning to the Bay Area scene of their younger days, 1956-1957 were important years for all involved; Wieners continued to publish the group—alongside his Black Mountain College colleagues Edward Dorn, Michael Rumaker, Jonathan Williams, and Fielding Dawson—in *Measure*. The magazine's second issue placed Jonas beside Jack Kerouac and Robert Duncan. After being incarcerated in Danbury, Connecticut for six months on a mail fraud charge, Jonas was again being published, this time by Amiri Baraka (then LeRoi Jones) and his wife Hettie in *Yugen* 8, where Jonas placed his "A Long Poem for Jack Spicer," a poem that includes the kind of caricatures of Jews common to Spicer and Jonas's writing going back to 1956, as Ellingham and Killian show. Whether Jonas's anti-Semitism originated with the attitudes of an adoptive white parent, as his notebooks allude to, or derive from his devotion to Ezra Pound, whose recordings he listened to on high rotation, is unknown; but Pound—as can be seen in Gregory Barnhisel's 2005 book *James Laughlin, New Directions, and the Remaking of Ezra Pound*—was held up as the preeminent master of Modernist letters despite his wartime support for Mussolini and infamous radio broadcasts.[12] Unlike other poets, perhaps, who could cherrypick from Pound's ideas and work, Jonas, in his unraveling mental state, was unable to filter the toxins, and he imbibed not only Pound's methods of composing poetry, but also Pound's valorizing of old, agrarian America, his fraught leaps of logic, his willful refusal to distinguish between banking corporations and the Jewish people. Jonas was uniquely ill-equipped to discern what might've been useful from what was certainly harmful.

As Jonas reached forty he encountered a poet seven years his junior who became a significant influence on him, Gerrit Lansing. Like some of Jonas's earliest connections, Lansing was of an Ivy League, patrician background. After studying magic with Stefan Walewski in New York (a connection made for Lansing by his and Walewski's mutual friend, song writer John LaTouche), Lansing moved to Abbadia Mare, now the Hammond Castle Museum, a granite castle built by inventor John Hays Hammond Jr. on the rocky coast of Gloucester, Massachusetts. From there, Lansing deepened his study of Aleister Crowley, publishing two issues of his literary magazine SET, combining his occult and poetic interests; in SET Jonas was published alongside Charles Olson, Kenward Elmslie, Diane Wakoski, and Robert Kelly, among others; the first issue included excerpts from Crowley's The Book of Lies (1912). In looking through Jonas's notebooks it could only have been from Lansing that Jonas received his elaborate reading list of occult volumes, many in French: Henri Serouya's La Kabbale (1947), Marcellin Berthelot's Les Origines de l'alchimie (1885), Jean Marquès-Rivière's Amulettes, talismans et pantacles (1938), Francis Barrett's The Magus (1801), Mircea Eliade's Cosmos and History (1954), Thomas Norton's Ordinal of Alchemy (1477), as well as works on John Dee, and Crowley's The Book of Thoth (1944), among many other titles.

Jonas was drawn to all manner of occult explanations; political, economic, and religious counternarratives, buried philosophical traditions, as well as divination and Tarot. He was a secret-keeper obsessed by the idea secrets were being kept from American voters and consumers, from the religious faithful. Suppressed truths could be deciphered, he felt, if only he'd listen hard enough. Magic arose again in "Magic Evenings" hosted at his apartments, culturally subterranean gatherings in a city of notoriously academicized high culture. These Evenings drew together poets from Boston and beyond, including Carol Weston and longstanding friend Raffael De Gruttola.

According to his death certificate Jonas died from a Glutethimide overdose, a drug, once common, now essentially withdrawn from the market due to its substantial side effects: the chimeras of Jonas's mind, the cognitive convulsions of his later thinking, might've been linked to the drug as much as to illness. Jonas came to fear lonesomeness, what he might do if relegated to his own devices. A page left for his last roommate reads: "Please don't leave me today I'm afraid to stay alone Please."

Stephen Jonas evaded society's definitions throughout his life, sly and mercurial to the last. Whether he made the long trek north from Georgia to New Jersey as part of the Great Migration, or was ripped from his Catholic Cabo Verdean or Puerto Rican culture, placed with Protestant whites, whether he was a practicing Quaker or Christian Scientist, whether he was Jones or Jonas or Santos, he was a poet. And the Boston demimonde of poets, addicts, and scammers came to be the only consistent human support in his life besides bureaucracies and asylums. Perhaps—just perhaps—he was Edward Jones, an African American ward of the state who appears on the 1930 census, born in 1921 to unknown parents, raised in Cambridge, Massachusetts by a U.S. Customs House clerk.[13] A boy without an inherited past, who forged and discarded makeshift histories as it suited him. We may never know. What matters is the achievement of his poems, his music of sorrow, anger, and passion.

David Rich, 2018

Endnotes

[1] hcl.harvard.edu/poetryroom/listeningbooth/.

[2] For instance, Thomas S. Jonas of Mashpee, Massachusetts, who was born in 1876, was categorized as "mulatto" on the 1880 census and "Indian" on the 1900. Year: 1880; Census Place: *Mashpee, Barnstable, Massachusetts*; Roll: 519; Page: 82A; Enumeration District: 005, in *Tenth Census of the United States, 1880* and Year: 1900; Census Place: *Mashpee, Barnstable, Massachusetts*; Page 2; Enumeration District: 0012; FHL microfilm: 1240631 in *Twelfth Census of the United States, 1900*. NB: vital records cited in this postscript were accessed via Ancestry.com in June, 2018. Ancestry.com. Provo, UT, USA: Ancestry.com Operations Inc.

[3] Year: 1930; Census Place: *New Bedford, Bristol, Massachusetts*; Page 7B; Enumeration District: 0119; FHL microfilm: 2340626 in Fifteenth Census of the United States, 1930.

[4] Jonas, Stephen. *Selected Poems*. Hoboken, NJ: Talisman House, 1994. p. 237.

[5] See the family of German-American printing press factory employee Peter Jonas. Year: 1990; Census Place: *Plainfield Ward 4, Union, New Jersey*; Page: 5; Enumeration District: 0129; FHL microfilm: 1240997, in *Twelfth Census of the United States, 1900* and Year: 1920; Census Place: *Plainfield Ward 1, Union, New Jersey*; Roll: T625_1071; Page 9B; Enumeration District: 118, in *Fourteenth Census of the United States, 1920*.

[6] Year: 1940; Census Place: *Plainfield, Union, New Jersey*; Roll: m-t0627-02387; Page: 9B; Enumeration District: 20-69A, in *Sixteenth Census of the United States, 1940*. See also listing for "Glickman, Louis (Nancy M) chiropractor 352 E Front h do" in *Polk's Plainfield (Union County, N.J.) City Directory 1944*. Pittsburgh, PA: R.L. Polk & Co., 1944.

[7] Year: 1940; Census Place: *Boston, Suffolk, Massachusetts*; Roll: m-t0627-01662; Page: 7B; Enumeration District: 15-166, in *Sixteenth Census of the United States, 1940*.

[8] Shand-Tucci, Douglass. *The Crimson Letter: Harvard, Homosexuality, and the Shaping of American Culture*. New York, NY: St. Martin's Press, 2003.

[9] For a taste of the Barn's activities during its heyday, see *Boston Globe* issues: Nov. 6, 1927; Dec. 22, 1929; Jan. 29, 1931; Mar. 26, 1931; Jan. 18, 1936; Dec. 11, 1928; Nov. 9, 1940; Nov. 13, 1941; May 7, 1942.

[10] Under Peabody heading, see: "—Avery S bookseller 124 Mt Vernon h do"

in *Polk's Boston (Suffolk County, Mass.) City Directory, 1948-49*. Vol. CXLIV. Boston, MA: R.L. Polk & Co., 1949. Avery Peabody's father, Ellery Peabody, was indeed a leather manufacturer, see: Year: 1920; Census Place: *Newton Ward 3, Middlesex, Massachusetts*; Roll: T625_716; Page: 2A; Enumeration District: 369, in *Fourteenth Census of the United States, 1920*.

[11] Ellingham, Lewis and Kevin Killian. *Poet Be Like God*. Hanover, NH: Wesleyan University Press, 1998, pp. 66-75.

[12] Barnhisel, Gregory. *James Laughlin, New Directions, and the Remaking of Ezra Pound*. Amherst, MA: University of Massachusetts Press, 2005.

[13] The 1930 Federal Census shows that 52-year old African-American U.S. Customs clerk Leigh Carter, a resident of Cambridge, Massachusetts, and his widowed, Virginia-born mother Maria, were raising three African-American wards of the state of unknown birth and origin, including 9-year old Edward Jones. Year: 1930; Census Place: *Cambridge, Middlesex, Massachusetts*; Page 1A; Enumeration District: 0049; FHL microfilm: 2340651, in *Fifteenth Census of the United States, 1930*.

Beginning in the 1950s until his death at age 49, **Stephen Jonas** (1921-1970) was an influential if underground figure of the New American Poetry. A gay African American poet of self-obscured origins, heavily influenced by Ezra Pound and Charles Olson, the Boston-based Jonas was a pioneer of the serial poem and mentor to such acknowledged masters as Jack Spicer and John Wieners. Major publications include *Love, the Poem, the Sea & Other Pieces Examined by Me* (1957), *Transmutations* (1966), *Exercises for Ear* (1968), and *Selected Poems* (1994).

Garrett Caples is a poet and an editor for City Lights, where he curates the Spotlight Poetry Series. He's written three books of poems and a book of essays, and edited or co-edited books by Philip Lamantia, Frank Lima, Richard O. Moore, Samuel Greenberg, and Penelope Rosemont.

Derek Fenner is an artist, educator, poet, and researcher. He earned his MFA in writing and poetics from the Jack Kerouac School of Disembodied Poetics at Naropa University. In 2000, with Ryan Gallagher, he co-founded Bootstrap Press, which has published over 40 books by poets across the country.

David Rich is the editor of *Charles Olson: Letters Home, 1949-1969* (Cape Ann Museum, 2010).

Joseph Torra is a poet, novelist, and editor. He edited *Selected Poems* by Stephen Jonas (Talisman, 1994).